Developing TACTICS for LISTENING

THIRD EDITION

More listening. More testing. More effective.

Jack C. Richards
with Grant Trew

OXFORD
UNIVERSITY PRESS

OXFORD
UNIVERSITY PRESS

198 Madison Avenue
New York, NY 10016 USA

Great Clarendon Street, Oxford OX2 6DP UK

Oxford University Press is a department of the University of Oxford. It furthers the University's objective of excellence in research, scholarship, and education by publishing worldwide in

Oxford New York

Auckland Cape Town Dar es Salaam Hong Kong Karachi Kuala Lumpur Madrid Melbourne Mexico City Nairobi New Delhi Shanghai Taipei Toronto

With offices in

Argentina Austria Brazil Chile Czech Republic France Greece Guatemala Hungary Italy Japan Poland Portugal Singapore South Korea Switzerland Thailand Turkey Ukraine Vietnam

OXFORD and OXFORD ENGLISH are registered trademarks of Oxford University Press in certain countries.

General Manager: Laura Pearson
Editorial Director, International Schools and Adult: Pam Murphy
Executive Publishing Manager: Erik Gundersen
Associate Editor: Jonathan Bucchino
Director, ADP: Susan Sanguily
Executive Design Manager: Maj-Britt Hagsted
Designer (cover and interior): Debbie Lofaso
Electronic Production Manager: Julie Armstrong
Image Manager: Trisha Masterson
Production Coordinator: Elizabeth Matsumoto
Senior Manufacturing Controller: Eve Wong

ISBN: 978-0-19-401385-7

Printed in China

This book is printed on paper from certified and well-managed sources.

13

ACKNOWLEDGMENTS

The authors and publisher are grateful to those who have given permission to reproduce the following extracts and adaptations of copyright material:

Illustrations by: Anita Romeo: 87; Christian Musselman: 19, 47, 54; Chris Pavely: 4, 20, 56, 64, 92; Element-Thomson: 58, 82; Geo Parkin: 98,103,106; Jacquie O'Neill: 26, 74; John Courtney: 66; Jon Keegan: 8, 36, 52, 72, 91; Kenneth Batelman: 109; Nina Edwards: 39; Terry Wong: 30.

Commissioned photography by: Gareth Boden; pg. 2 (talking); Chris King; pg. 50 (basketball).

The publishers would like to thank the following for their kind permission to reproduce photographs: Valueline / Punchstock; pg. 2 (watching TV); Fancy / Alamy; pg. 2 (football); John Eder / Getty Images; pg. 3 (movie); Toby Burrows / Digital Vision; pg. 6 (paying bus); Cultura / Punchstock; pg. 6 (subway); Linda Matlow / Alamy; pg. 6 (ticket window); B.O'Kane / Alamy; pg. 6 (airline counter); Peter Titmuss / Alamy; pg. 6 (ferry landing); Pegaz / Alamy; pg. 6 (taxi); Blend Images / Alamy; pg. 7 (calling); Greg Ceo / Getty Images; pg. 7 (taxi counter); Somos Images / Photolibrary.com; pg. 10 (man waving); Blend Images / Punchstock; pg. 10 (woman waving); SW Productions / Getty Images; pg. 11 (helping); Dimitri Vervitsiotis / Getty Images; pg. 12 (peaking); Photodisc / Punchstock; pg. 14 (potluck); Comstock; pg. 14 (barbeque); Pixland / Punchstock; pg. 15 (door); Cultura / Punchstock; pg. 15 (cat); Polka Dot / Punchstock; pg. 15 (talking); Comstock / Punchstock; pg. 15 (looking at painting); Comstock / Punchstock; pg. 15 (video game); Südstern Südstern / photolibrary.com; pg. 15 (piano); Mlenny / iStockphoto; pg. 16 (barbeque); B. Tanaka / Getty Images; pg. 18 (restaurant); Radius Images / Alamy; pg. 18 (eating); AVAVA / Shutterstock; pg. 22 (gift); EuToch / iStockphoto; pg. 22 (pen); Photodisc; pg. 22 (flowers); emily2k / iStockphoto; pg. 22 (bracelet); AndyL / iStockphoto; pg. 22 (neck tie); Tomas Bercic / iStockphoto; pg. 22 (teapot); wladimir Bulgar isolated / Alamy; pg. 22 (key chain); i love images / Alamy; pg. 23 (store window); Mel Yates / Getty Images; pg. 24 (candy counter); Digital Vision / Punchstock; pg. 27 (flight attendant); Ilja Mašík / Shutterstock; pg. 28 (airplane); Flying Colours Ltd / Getty Images; pg. 30 (eating); Fuse / Getty Images; pg. 31 (dropped); Blend Images / Alamy; pg. 32 (texting in rain); PhotoAlto/James Hardy; pg. 34 (window washer); Pixland / Jupiterimages / Punchstock; pg. 34 (architect); Image Source / Punchstock; pg. 34 (lecture); Valueline / Punchstock; pg. 34 (book store); Rob Walls / Alamy; pg. 34 (hair stylist); Image Source / Punchstock; pg. 34 (flight attendant); comosaydice / Shutterstock; pg. 34 (car mechanic); Arthur S. Aubry / Photodisc; pg. 35 (baker); Andrea Chu / Punchstock; pg. 35 (bellhop); Silvrshootr / iStockphoto; pg. 38 (sit ups); PhotoLink / Photodisc; pg. 40 (biking); Christopher Futcher / iStockphoto; pg. 42 (asking out); MBI / Alamy; pg. 43 (talking); Kharidehal Abhirama Ashwin / Shutterstock; pg. 44 (on phone); Getty Images; pg. 46 (lunch line); Corbis Premium RF / Alamy; pg. 46 (working out); Patrick Clark / Photodisc; pg. 46 (classroom); Manfred Rutz / Getty Images; pg. 46 (advisor); Image Source; pg. 46 (library); Mira / Alamy; pg. 46 (bookstore); Corel; pg. 48 (campus); Fuse / Punchstock; pg. 50 (basball); Rainer and Simone Hoffmann / Alamy; pg. 50 (reading); cmfotoworks / Shutterstock; pg. 50 (stamps); Pete Pahham / Shutterstock; pg. 50 (gardening); Todd Keith / iStockphoto; pg. 50 (eating); Ferenc Szelepcsenyi / Shutterstock; pg. 50 (orchestra); Moodboard / photolibrary.com; pg. 51 (painter); Blend Images / Punchstock; pg. 51 (gardening); creatas / Punchstock.com; pg. 54 (washing); Plush Studios / Getty Images; pg. 55 (returning shirt); Jupiterimages / Getty Images; pg. 58 (calling); Inspirestock / Punchstock; pg. 59 (checking in); Pierre-Yves Babelon / Shutterstock; pg. 60 (resort); Moviestore collection Ltd / Alamy; pg. 62 (Up); Moviestore collection Ltd / Alamy; pg. 62 (Iron Man); prism68 / Shutterstock; pg. 66 (construction); Jupiterimages / Getty Images; pg. 66 (roller coaster); Andersen Ross / Getty Images; pg. 67 (afraid in car); Cultura / Punchstock; pg. 68 (afraid of elevator); Heath Korvola / Getty Images; pg. 70 (texting); Yellow Dog Productions / Getty Images; pg. 71 (on phone); Image Source; pg. 74 (museum); Life File Photo Library Ltd / Alamy; pg. 75 (tour bus); E.J. Baumeister Jr. / Alamy; pg. 76 (boy); B.O'Kane / Alamy; pg. 78 (newstand); Jack Hollingsworth / Getty Images; pg. 78 (airline counter); KAKIMAGE / Alamy; pg. 78 (baggage); dbimages / Alamy; pg. 78 (currency exchange); Wm. Baker / GhostWorx Images / Alamy; pg. 78 (restroom); Corbis Premium RF / Alamy; pg. 78 (ticket counter); [apply pictures] / Alamy; pg. 78 (taxi); Mike Chinery / Alamy; pg. 78 (bus stop); Ryan McVay / Getty Images; pg. 79 (ticket counter); dbimages / Alamy; pg. 80 (airport); charles taylor / Shutterstock; pg. 82 (passport); Hola Images / Punchstock; pg. 82 (male); Photodisc / Punchstock; pg. 83 (guest counter); hxdbzxy / Shutterstock; pg. 84 (hotel room); l to r Kent Knudson/PhotoLink / Photodisc; pg. 86 (heavy traffic); Elena Elisseeva / Shutterstock; pg. 86 (light traffic); Dmitry Kalinovsky / Shutterstock; pg. 86 (road repair); Evgeny Murtola; pg. 86 (car accident); cw from top Hisham Ibrahim / Getty Images; pg. 86 (traffic); Darryl Brooks / Shutterstock; pg. 86 (road closed); Paul Gardner / iStockphoto; pg. 86 (barricades); Jack Dagley Photography / Shutterstock; pg. 86 (car accident); Glowimages / Punchstock; pg. 86 (bridge); Image Source / Alamy; pg. 86 (traffic); Masterfile.com; pg. 88 (bus); Purestock / Alamy; pg. 90 (dorm); MBI / Alamy; pg. 90 (cleaning); Mlenny / iStockphoto; pg. 94 (running); Photodisc; pg. 94 (water fall); rantisekhojdysz / Shutterstock; pg. 94 (reef); Ilene MacDonald / Alamy; pg. 94 (towing); Medioimages/Photodisc / Getty Images; pg. 94 (hula); Douglas Peebles Photography / Alamy; pg. 94 (volcano); Gaertner / Alamy; pg. 94 (car on road); Full House Images / Getty Images; pg. 95 (Eifle Tower); Gabrielle Revere/Getty Images; pg. 99 (student); mangostock / Shutterstock; pg. 100 (waiter); corepics / Shutterstock; pg. 100 (cooking); Tom Grill / Shutterstock; pg. 100 (present); Dmitriy Shironosov / Shutterstock; pg. 100 (flight attendant); Anna Lurye / Shutterstock; pg. 100 (airport); Tommaso79 / Shutterstock; pg. 100 (car problem); Masterfile; pg. 101 (student); David Davis Photoproductions RF/Alamy; pg. 103 (student); David Huntley / Shutterstock; pg. 104 (gardening); Lubo / Shutterstock; pg. 104 (reading); Tomasz Nieweglowski / Shutterstock; pg. 104 (kite); Dmitrijs Dmitrijevs / Shutterstock; pg. 104 (hotel desk); Alex Hinds / Shutterstock; pg. 104 (bed); Deklofenak / Shutterstock; pg. 104 (movie); Corbis/Photolibrary; pg. 105 (student); David Davis Photoproductions RF/Alamy; pg. 107 (student); Corbis/Photolibrary; pg. 109 (student); D. Hurst/Alamy, back cover (mp3 player).

TACTICS FOR LISTENING

THIRD EDITION

More listening. More testing. More effective.

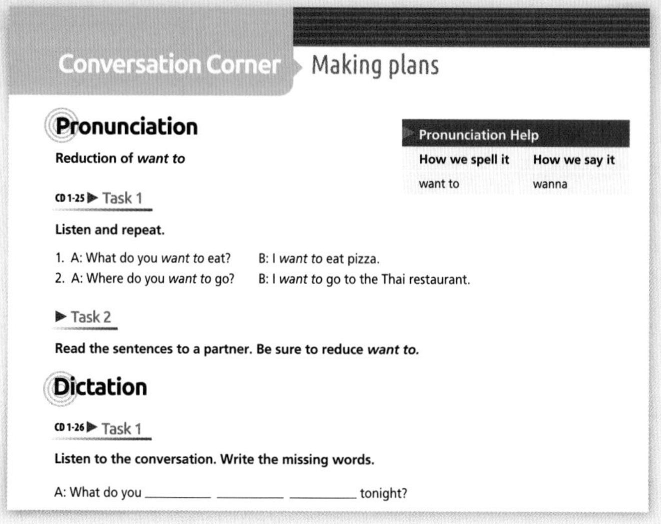
Conversation Corner | Making plans

Pronunciation

Reduction of *want to*

Pronunciation Help	
How we spell it	**How we say it**
want to	wanna

CD 1-25 ▶ Task 1

Listen and repeat.

1. A: What do you *want to* eat? B: I *want to* eat pizza.
2. A: Where do you *want to* go? B: I *want to* go to the Thai restaurant.

▶ Task 2

Read the sentences to a partner. Be sure to reduce *want to*.

Dictation

CD 1-26 ▶ Task 1

Listen to the conversation. Write the missing words.

A: What do you ________ ________ ________ tonight?

More listening

40% more listening activities than before!

ALL-NEW Conversation Corner pages provide **Pronunciation** and **Dictation** activities for oral production and listening comprehension practice.

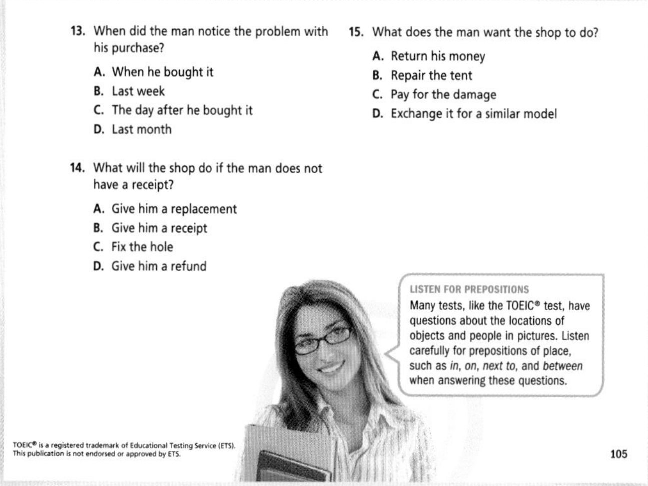
13. When did the man notice the problem with his purchase?
    - A. When he bought it
    - B. Last week
    - C. The day after he bought it
    - D. Last month
14. What will the shop do if the man does not have a receipt?
    - A. Give him a replacement
    - B. Give him a receipt
    - C. Fix the hole
    - D. Give him a refund
15. What does the man want the shop to do?
    - A. Return his money
    - B. Repair the tent
    - C. Pay for the damage
    - D. Exchange it for a similar model

LISTEN FOR PREPOSITIONS
Many tests, like the TOEIC® test, have questions about the locations of objects and people in pictures. Listen carefully for prepositions of place, such as *in*, *on*, *next to*, and *between* when answering these questions.

TOEIC® is a registered trademark of Educational Testing Service (ETS). This publication is not endorsed or approved by ETS.

105

More testing

ALL-NEW Tactics for Testing section teaches test-taking skills and presents six practice tests in the style of the TOEIC® test and other exams.

ALL-NEW Testing Program and Resource CD-ROM provides midterm and final tests in the style of the TOEIC® test and other exams to help students prepare for success.

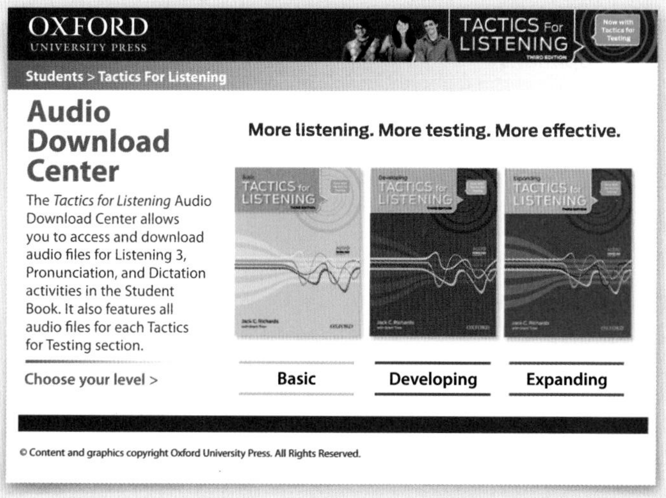
OXFORD UNIVERSITY PRESS

TACTICS For LISTENING THIRD EDITION

Now with Tactics for Testing

Students > Tactics For Listening

Audio Download Center

More listening. More testing. More effective.

The *Tactics for Listening* Audio Download Center allows you to access and download audio files for Listening 3, Pronunciation, and Dictation activities in the Student Book. It also features all audio files for each Tactics for Testing section.

Choose your level > | Basic | Developing | Expanding

© Content and graphics copyright Oxford University Press. All Rights Reserved.

More effective

ALL-NEW Audio Download Center

At www.oup.com/elt/tacticsforlistening3e, students can download selected Student Book audio for anytime, anywhere self-study.

Scope and Sequence

Unit	Topic	Listening Skills	Pronunciation & Dictation	Conversation
1 The Weekend page 2	Past events	• Listening for details • Listening for opinions • Listening for key words	Past *–ed* verb endings	Talking about the weekend
2 City Transportation page 6	Taxis, trains, and buses	• Listening for locations • Listening for numbers • Listening for details	Intonation of *Wh-* questions	Asking about transportation
3 Neighbors page 10	Getting along with neighbors	• Listening for reasons • Listening for details • Listening for opinions • Listening for gist	Word stress in compound nouns	Neighborhood gossip
4 Celebrations page 14	Meals and get-togethers	• Listening for key words • Listening for gist • Listening for details	Reduction of *Wh-* + *do you*	Planning a celebration
5 Restaurants page 18	Food and going out to eat	• Listening for locations • Listening for details • Listening for opinions • Listening for gist	Reduction of *want to*	Making plans
6 Gifts page 22	Shopping and department stores	• Listening for details • Listening for decisions • Listening for opinions • Listening for gist	Syllable stress in names	Buying a gift

Unit	Topic	Listening Skills	Pronunciation & Dictation	Conversation
7 Air Travel page 26	Instructions for flying	• Listening for gist • Listening for details • Listening for opinions	Reduction of *could you* and *would you*	Preparing for takeoff
8 Mishaps page 30	Problems and solutions	• Listening for gist • Listening for details • Listening for solutions	Reduction of *did you*	Describing a mishap
9 Jobs page 34	Life at work	• Listening for gist • Listening for key words • Listening for details	Intonation of yes/no questions	Describing jobs
10 Keeping Fit page 38	Fitness and exercise	• Listening for details • Listening for reasons • Listening for topics	Reduction of *used to* and *use to*	Asking about past actions
11 Invitations page 42	Accepting or refusing an invitation	• Listening for invitations • Listening for acceptances and refusals • Listening for details	Reduction of *Do you* and *Are you*	Giving an invitation
12 Campus Life page 46	Teachers, classes, and campus	• Listening for locations • Listening for details • Listening for gist • Listening for opinions	Intonation of words in a series	Describing likes and dislikes

Scope and Sequence

Unit	Topic	Listening Skills	Pronunciation & Dictation	Conversation
13 Hobbies and Pastimes page 50	Interests	• Listening for gist • Listening for details • Listening for likes and dislikes	Syllable stress in words	Talking about hobbies
14 Shopping Problems page 54	Returning items	• Listening for gist • Listening for details • Listening for opinions	Reduction of *need to* and *like to*	Returning an item
15 Hotel Services page 58	Staying in a hotel	• Listening for details • Listening for key words • Listening for opinions	Reduction of the vowel sound in *can*	Asking for help
16 Movies page 62	Movie types	• Listening for key words • Listening for times • Listening for opinions • Listening for recommendations	Linked sounds *s* and *z*	Talking about movies
17 Fears page 66	Being afraid	• Listening for gist • Listening for details • Listening for problems	Sentence stress	Describing fears
18 Phone Messages page 70	Voicemails	• Listening for information • Listening for details	Intonation of phone numbers	Saying phone numbers

Scope and Sequence

Units	Testing Focus	Test-taking Skill	Tasks
1 – 4 page 98	Focused listening	Establishing the main idea	• Answering picture-based questions • Matching statements with the appropriate response • Comprehension questions based on short conversations
5 – 8 page 100	Listening for details	Taking notes as you listen	• Matching statements with a photograph • Matching questions with the appropriate response • Comprehension questions based on a conversation
9 – 12 page 102	Listening for organization	Listening for transitional words	• Completing notes based on a conversation • Completing a map based on a talk
13 – 16 page 104	Picture-based questions	Listening for prepositions	• Matching statements with a photograph • Matching questions with the appropriate response • Comprehension questions based on a conversation
17 – 20 page 106	Listening for details	Listening for paraphrasing	• Answering picture-based questions • Matching statements with the appropriate response • Comprehension questions based on short conversations
21 – 24 page 108	Question-focused listening	Preparing for the test day	• Completing notes based on a conversation • Completing a map based on a talk

Series Overview

Tactics for Listening Third Edition is a three-level series of listening textbooks for English learners, comprehensively revised and expanded to provide more listening input and a new focus on developing test-taking skills. The three *Tactics for Listening* levels—Basic, Developing, and Expanding—comprise a comprehensive course in listening skills.

Developing Tactics for Listening

Developing Tactics for Listening is the second level of the *Tactics for Listening* series. It is intended for pre-intermediate students who have studied English previously but need further practice in understanding everyday conversational language. There are 24 units, four of which contain completely new content for the Third Edition. *Developing Tactics for Listening* can be used as the main text for a listening course, as a complementary text in a conversation course, or as the basis for structured student self-study.

Each unit features a topic that relates to everyday life such as transportation, neighbors, or campus life. The topics have been chosen for their frequency in conversation and their interest to learners. A wide variety of stimulating and useful activities is included to give students graded practice in listening.

Student Book

In the *Developing Tactics for Listening* Student Book, students practice listening for a variety of purposes and hear examples of different types of spoken English including casual conversations, instructions, directions, requests, descriptions, apologies, and suggestions. Essential listening skills are practiced throughout the text. These skills include listening for key words, details, and gist; listening and making inferences; listening for attitudes; listening to questions and responding; and recognizing and identifying information.

Each unit has five sections. The first section, *Getting Ready*, introduces the topic of the unit and presents key vocabulary for the unit listening tasks. The next three sections, *Listening 1*, *Listening 2*, and *Listening 3* are linked to conversations or monologues on the audio program. The *Listening* sections provide task-based, graded listening practice. The final section, *Conversation Corner*, allows students to move from receptive to productive use of language through structured *Pronunciation*, *Dictation*, and *Conversation* practice. All of the *Conversation Corner* content is completely new for the Third Edition.

Tactics for Testing, an all-new review and extension section at the end of each Student Book, provides additional listening comprehension practice through two-page lessons. These *Tactics for Testing* materials help students develop better test-taking skills while exposing them to formats from the listening sections of the TOEIC® test, the TOEFL® test, IELTS™, and other exams. A Testing Focus and Test-taking Skill for each lesson help students and teachers get the greatest benefit from *Tactics for Testing*.

A complete Vocabulary Index is also provided in the back of each Student Book.

Audio Program

The complete audio program for the *Developing Tactics for Listening* Student Book is available as a set of four Class Audio CDs.

AUDIO DOWNLOAD

New for the Third Edition, the audio tracks for the *Listening 3*, *Pronunciation*, and *Dictation* activities in each unit as well as audio for the *Tactics for Testing* section at the back of the book are also available to students and teachers for download at www.oup.com/elt/tacticsforlistening3e, providing anytime, anywhere listening practice and opportunities for self-study.

Teacher's Book

The *Developing Tactics for Listening* Teacher's Book provides teaching notes, answer keys, optional activities, audio scripts, and photocopiable Vocabulary Worksheets for each unit. An icon at the bottom of the first page of each Student Book unit reminds teachers that there is a Vocabulary Worksheet available for that unit.

Testing Program and Resource CD-ROM

Packaged with the Teacher's Book, the *Developing Tactics for Listening* Testing Program and Resource CD-ROM contains reproducible unit quizzes and midterm and final tests. New for the Third Edition, midterm and final tests are also available in the TOEIC® test, the TOEFL® test, and IELTS™ formats as well as in the formats of other major English exams. The Testing Program and Resource CD-ROM also contains reproducible Conversation Worksheets to facilitate additional unit-closing activities.

UNIT 1

The Weekend

Getting Ready

What did you do last weekend? Check (✓) your answers and compare them with a partner.

- ☐ went to a movie
- ☐ went to the gym
- ☐ played a sport
- ☐ met a friend
- ☐ watched TV
- ☐ watched a DVD
- ☐ went on a date
- ☐ went to a nightclub
- ☐ played computer games

Asking about the weekend

CD 1-2 Listening 1

What did these people do last weekend? Listen and circle the correct answer.

1. She __________.
   a. went to a club
   b. watched TV

2. He __________.
   a. met a girl
   b. went to his sister's house

3. He __________.
   a. went to the gym
   b. entered a bodybuilding competition

4. He __________.
   a. played with his nephews
   b. went out with a friend

5. She __________.
   a. went to a party
   b. went to a movie

6. She __________.
   a. watched a DVD
   b. watched baseball on TV

Vocabulary Worksheet

Listening 2

CD 1-3 ▶ Task 1

Did these people enjoy their weekend? Listen and check (✓) the correct answer.

	Yes	No
1.	☐	☑
2.	☐	☐
3.	☐	☐
4.	☐	☐
5.	☐	☐
6.	☐	☐

CD 1-3 ▶ Task 2

Listen again. What did each person do on the weekend? Circle the correct answer.

1. He __________.

- **a.** watched a science program on TV
- **b.** played video games
- **(c.)** went to a movie

2. He __________.

- **a.** stayed at home
- **b.** went to the beach for the weekend
- **c.** went to the mountains

3. He __________.

- **a.** read lots of interesting magazines
- **b.** used the computer
- **c.** read an interesting book

4. She __________.

- **a.** played in a band
- **b.** went to a concert
- **c.** played tennis

5. She __________.

- **a.** stayed home and watched TV
- **b.** studied for an exam
- **c.** went out with friends

6. She __________.

- **a.** visited friends
- **b.** went to the countryside
- **c.** went out with friends

Listening 3

CD 1-4 ▶ Task 1

How was each person's weekend? Listen and circle the correct answer.

1. a. so-so	2. a. disappointing	3. a. tiring	4. a. awful
b. terrible	b. pleasant	b. terrific	b. quiet
(c.) great	c. boring	c. wonderful	c. enjoyable

CD 1-4 ▶ Task 2

Listen again. Are these statements true or false? Check (✓) the correct answer.

		True	False
1.	a. She won a contest in a music store.	☐	☑
	b. She won a trip to Las Vegas.	☐	☐
2.	a. They went to a restaurant for dinner.	☐	☐
	b. His friend has a very interesting job.	☐	☐
3.	a. The park is very far from town.	☐	☐
	b. They didn't see any wild birds or butterflies on the trip.	☐	☐
4.	a. There were a lot of interesting people at the party.	☐	☐
	b. The party ended early.	☐	☐

Talking about the weekend

Pronunciation

Past tense –*ed* endings

Pronunciation Help

Sounds like /t/	Sounds like /d/	Sounds like /id/
finished	played	visited
helped	traveled	waited
watched	stayed	needed

CD 1-5 ▶ Task 1

Listen and repeat.

1. I lik*ed* the movie.
2. I studi*ed* for a test.
3. She stay*ed* with us.
4. We want*ed* to go home.

▶ Task 2

Read the sentences to a partner. Be sure to pronounce the past –*ed* verb endings correctly.

Dictation

CD 1-6 ▶ Task 1

Listen to the conversation. Write the missing words.

A: Hi, Amy. What did you do this weekend?

B: Oh, not much. I __________ home and __________ on a project.

A: Is that all?

B: No. I also finished a good book. Later, I __________ __________ __________. What about you?

A: I played tennis. The courts were crowded. I __________ a long time to play!

B: What else did you do?

A: Some friends __________ __________ to dinner. Later, we went to a club and met a lot of __________ __________.

▶ Task 2

Practice the conversation with a partner. Be sure to pronounce the past –*ed* verb endings correctly.

Conversation

Work in pairs. What did you do last weekend? Ask and answer questions about your weekend with your partner.

UNIT 2

City Transportation

Getting Ready

Check (✓) your own answers to the questions below and compare them with a partner.

How often do you use taxis?

- ☐ every day
- ☐ about once or twice a week
- ☐ not very often
- ☐ other: __________

When do you usually use taxis?

- ☐ when I am in a hurry
- ☐ when there isn't any other way to get somewhere
- ☐ when it is raining
- ☐ other: __________

How is the taxi service in your city?

☐ excellent ☐ very good ☐ okay ☐ poor

CD 1-7

Listening 1

People are talking about transportation. Listen and number the pictures.

A. ☐

B. 1

C. ☐

D. ☐

E. ☐

F. ☐

Vocabulary Worksheet

Listening 2

CD 1-8 ▶ Task 1

Four hotel guests are calling for a taxi. Are these statements true or false? Listen and check (✓) the correct answer.

	True	False
1. The caller's flight leaves in four hours.	☐	☑
2. The caller wants to go to another hotel.	☐	☐
3. The caller needs to catch a train.	☐	☐
4. The caller's friend is going to have a baby soon.	☐	☐

CD 1-8 ▶ Task 2

Listen again. How much will each ride cost? Circle the correct answer.

1. **a.** $14
(b.) $40

2. **a.** $12
b. $20

3. **a.** $15
b. $50

4. **a.** $18
b. $80

Listening 3

CD 1-9 ▶ Task 1

Visitors are talking about taxis. Listen and check (✓) their opinions about taxi service.

	Good	Okay	Not good
1.	☐	☐	☑
2.	☐	☐	☐
3.	☐	☐	☐
4.	☐	☐	☐

CD 1-9 ▶ Task 2

Listen again. Circle the correct answer.

1. The thing she hates the most is that the __________.
   - (a.) taxis aren't air-conditioned
   - b. drivers drive too fast
   - c. drivers are rude

2. The thing he likes the most is __________.
   - a. the prices
   - b. that the taxis are clean
   - c. the drivers

3. The thing he hates the most is that the __________.
   - a. taxis are too expensive
   - b. drivers don't speak English very well
   - c. taxis are not very safe

4. The thing she likes the most is that the __________.
   - a. taxis are comfortable
   - b. drivers speak English well
   - c. drivers take credit cards

Asking about transportation

Pronunciation

Intonation of *Wh-* questions

Pronunciation Help

Use falling intonation for *Wh-* questions.

CD 1-10 ▶ Task 1

Listen and repeat.

1. When does the train leave?
2. How far is it?
3. Where do you get the bus?
4. How much is the fare?
5. What time is your train?
6. How long is the flight?

▶ Task 2

Read the questions to a partner. Be sure to use the correct intonation.

Dictation

CD 1-11 ▶ Task 1

Listen to the conversation. Write the missing words.

A: Where do you get the bus __________ __________?

B: I don't take the bus.

A: Oh. How do you __________ __________ __________?

B: I take the subway.

A: How often do you __________ __________?

B: I take it every day.

A: How much __________ __________ __________?

B: It costs about $50 a month.

▶ Task 2

Practice the conversation with a partner. Be sure to use the correct intonation.

Conversation

Work in pairs. Think about how you get to school. Ask each other about the ways you get to school.

UNIT 3

Neighbors

Getting Ready

What makes a good neighbor or a bad neighbor? Check (✓) your answers and compare them with a partner.

	Good	Bad
1. Borrows things and doesn't return them	☐	☐
2. Always says "hello" when you see them	☐	☐
3. Often plays loud music	☐	☐
4. Knows what everyone in the neighborhood is doing	☐	☐
5. Likes to gossip about other neighbors	☐	☐
6. Other: ________________	☐	☐

CD 1-12

Listening 1

People are talking about their neighbors. Listen and circle each person's opinion.

1. Bob thinks his neighbor is __________.
   a. fun
   (b.) inconsiderate

2. Jin-suk thinks his neighbors are __________.
   a. strange
   b. nice

3. Jennifer thinks her neighbor is __________.
   a. unfriendly
   b. shy

4. Douglas thinks his neighbor is __________.
   a. hardworking
   b. nosy

5. Susan thinks her neighbor is __________.
   a. helpful
   b. lonely

6. Robert thinks his neighbors are __________.
   a. responsible
   b. cheap

Listening 2

CD 1-13 ▶ Task 1

People are talking to their neighbors. Is each person making a request, an offer, or a complaint? Listen and check (✓) the correct answer.

	Offer	Request	Complaint
1.	☑	☐	☐
2.	☐	☐	☐
3.	☐	☐	☐
4.	☐	☐	☐
5.	☐	☐	☐
6.	☐	☐	☐

CD 1-13 ▶ Task 2

Listen again. Circle the correct statement.

1. **a.** Mrs. Coleman normally carries her own bags.
   (b.) The delivery driver isn't working today.
2. **a.** Today is Cindy's birthday.
   b. The painting is a gift from Cindy's brother.
3. **a.** Kyle needs to go to work.
   b. Mrs. Choi will ask her guests to move their cars.
4. **a.** Jack and Marissa have met before.
   b. Marissa's brother is supposed to help her move.
5. **a.** Hillary and her husband are going away for business.
   b. Hillary and her husband will be away for two weeks.
6. **a.** Ken has already returned Diane's punch bowl.
   b. Ken has borrowed other things that he hasn't returned.

Listening 3

CD 1-14 ▶ Task 1

People are describing their neighbors. Is each statement true or false? Listen and check (✓) the correct answer.

		True	False
1. a.	She doesn't like her neighbor now.	☐	☑
b.	Her neighbor is elderly.	☐	☐
2. a.	He trusts his neighbor.	☐	☐
b.	His neighbor still watches his children.	☐	☐
3. a.	Her neighbor is often impolite to her.	☐	☐
b.	She understands why her neighbor never accepts her invitations.	☐	☐
4. a.	The man has always disliked his neighbor.	☐	☐
b.	The man has tried to speak to his neighbor about the problem.	☐	☐

CD 1-14 ▶ Task 2

Listen again. What changed each person's opinion about their neighbor? Circle the correct answer.

1. **(a.)** Her neighbor stopped a burglar from robbing her house.
   b. Her neighbor moved away while she was on vacation.

2. **a.** His neighbor refused to watch his children.
   b. His neighbor forgot to pick up his children from day care.

3. **a.** Her neighbor finally accepted one of her invitations.
   b. She learned that her neighbor volunteers in his free time.

4. **a.** His neighbor won't mind his own business.
   b. His neighbor got a new and annoying hobby.

Conversation Corner ▸ Neighborhood gossip

Pronunciation

Word stress in compound nouns

Pronunciation Help

Stress the first syllable of the word in a compound noun.

CD 1-15 ▶ **Task 1**

Listen and repeat.

1. láw firm
2. púnch bowl
3. grócery bag
4. búsiness trip
5. máilbox key
6. dáy care

▶ **Task 2**

Read the words to a partner. Be sure to stress the correct syllable in each compound noun.

Dictation

CD 1-16 ▶ **Task 1**

Listen to the conversation. Write the missing words.

A: Did you hear about the argument between Steve and Mr. Riley?

B: An argument? But they've been friends for years. What happened?

A: Steve was cutting some __________ __________ from that tree in his yard, and one fell on the roof of Mr. Riley's car.

B: Oh, no! You know that car is his __________ __________.

A: Right. Well, Steve offered to take it to a __________ __________ and pay for the damages.

B: That __________ __________.

A: Yeah. But Mr. Riley was so angry that he won't even talk to Steve anymore.

▶ **Task 2**

Practice the conversation with a partner. Be sure to stress the correct syllable in each compound noun.

Conversation

Work in pairs. Think of a disagreement you've had with a neighbor. Tell your partner about it.

UNIT 4

Celebrations

Getting Ready

Match each meal or party on the left with the correct description on the right. Compare your answers with a partner.

1. potluck dinner _b_
2. birthday party ___
3. buffet ___
4. surprise party ___
5. barbecue ___
6. snack ___

a. A small, quick meal or something eaten between meals
b. A meal in which each guest brings a dish
c. A meal in which food is cooked outside on a grill
d. A party where a person is given gifts and a cake with candles on it
e. A meal in which all the food is put out on a table and guests serve themselves
f. A party that the guest of honor knows nothing about

CD 1-17 Listening 1

People are discussing parties. What kind of party are they talking about? Listen and circle the correct answer.

1. a. dinner party
   (b.) surprise party
2. a. potluck dinner
   b. barbecue
3. a. surprise party
   b. birthday party
4. a. buffet
   b. birthday party
5. a. buffet
   b. barbecue
6. a. potluck dinner
   b. buffet

Listening 2

CD 1-18 ▶ Task 1

People are talking at parties. Listen and number the pictures.

A. 

B. 

C. 

D. 

E. 

F. 

CD 1-18 ▶ Task 2

Listen again. Circle the correct answer.

1. (a.) The cake is homemade.
   b. The cake came from a store.
   c. A friend brought the cake.

2. a. He'll play now.
   b. He might play later.
   c. He doesn't play.

3. a. He bought the game recently.
   b. He played the game all day.
   c. He doesn't like the game.

4. a. She has brought the flowers for everyone.
   b. She has brought the flowers for the woman's husband.
   c. She has brought the flowers for the woman.

5. a. He bought it.
   b. It was a present.
   c. He painted it himself.

6. a. The cat isn't very friendly.
   b. The cat is very friendly.
   c. The cat is tired.

Listening 3

CD 1-19 ▶ Task 1

What did the people do at each party? Listen and circle the correct answer.

1. She ___________.
   a. played party games
   b. danced
   c. sang songs

2. He ___________.
   a. watched a home movie
   b. danced
   c. ate lots of food

3. She ___________.
   a. danced
   b. sang songs
   c. met old friends

4. He ___________.
   a. played games
   b. ate junk food
   c. listened to music

CD 1-19 ▶ Task 2

Listen again. What phrase completes each statement? Write the correct letter.

1. The best thing was _d_
2. The worst thing was ___
3. The best thing was ___
4. The worst thing was ___

a. she learned some Spanish songs.
b. there wasn't enough food.
c. no one brought music.
d. the music.

Conversation Corner Planning a celebration

Pronunciation

Reduction of *Wh-* + *do you*

CD 1-20 ▶ Task 1

Listen and repeat.

1. *What do you* do?
2. *What do you* want?
3. *Where do you* live?
4. *How do you* do?

Pronunciation Help

How we spell it	How we say it
What do you	Whadaya
Where do you	Wheredaya
When do you	Whendaya
Who do you	Whodaya
How do you	Howdaya

▶ Task 2

Read the questions to a partner. Be sure to reduce *Wh* + *do you.*

Dictation

CD 1-21 ▶ Task 1

Listen to the conversation. Write the missing words.

A: __________ __________ __________ want to do for Brandon's birthday?

B: Let's have a party!

A: __________ __________ __________ want to have it?

B: How about Saturday night?

A: Okay. Where do you __________ __________ __________ it?

B: How about my place?

A: Sounds great. Now, __________ __________ __________ want to invite?

B: All of Brandon's friends!

▶ Task 2

Practice the conversation with a partner. Be sure to reduce *Wh* + *do you*.

Conversation

Work in pairs. Imagine you are having a party for a classmate.
Talk to your partner about the party plans.

TACTICS FOR TESTING
PAGE 98

UNIT 5

Restaurants

Getting Ready

What are your favorite kinds of restaurants? Check (✓) your answers and compare them with a partner.

☐ Thai	☐ Mexican	☐ Japanese	☐ fast food
☐ French	☐ Korean	☐ Chinese	☐ other: ________________

CD 1-22

Listening 1

Where do the people decide to eat? Listen and circle the correct answer.

1. a. Chinese restaurant
b. Fast Fried Chicken

2. a. Quick Burger
b. Pizza Pit

3. a. home
b. out

4. a. steak house
b. Korean restaurant

5. a. seafood restaurant
b. pizza restaurant

6. a. Mexican restaurant
b. Japanese restaurant

7. a. fast food restaurant
b. French restaurant

8. a. home
b. vegetarian restaurant

Listening 2

CD 1-23 ▶ Task 1

People are ordering food in a restaurant. What does each person order? Listen and check (✓) the correct picture.

1.

a. b.

2.
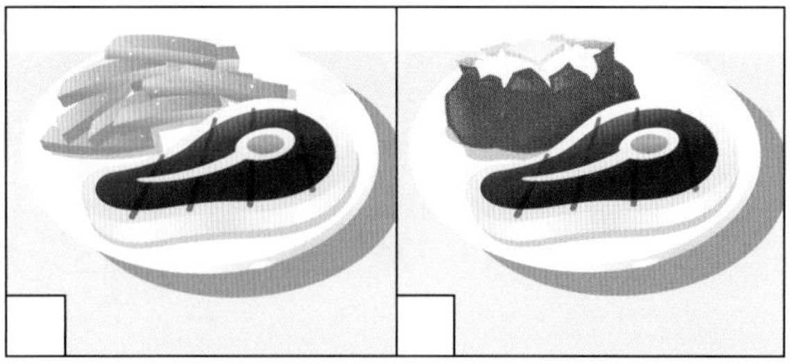
a. b.

3.
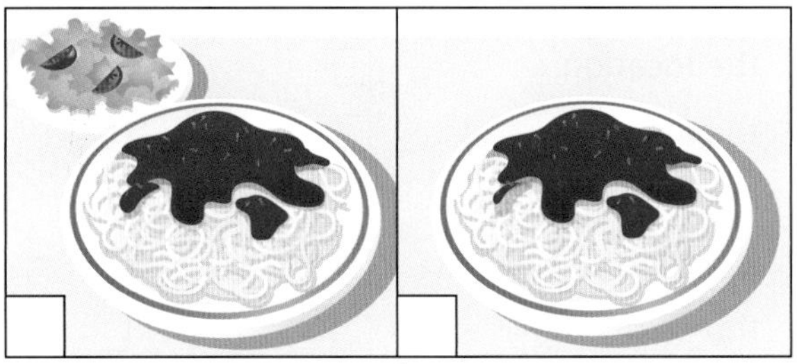
a. b.

4.

a. b.

5.
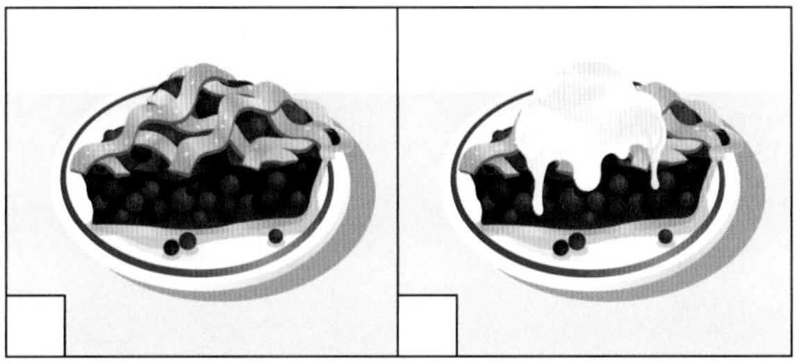
a. b.

6.
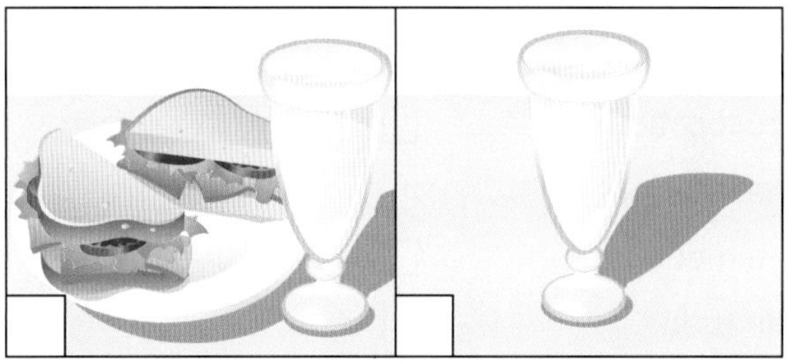
a. b.

CD 1-23 ▶ Task 2

Listen again. Are these statements true or false? Check (✓) the correct answer.

	True	False
1. The customer is not very hungry.	☐	☑
2. The customer loves fries.	☐	☐
3. The customer hates spicy food.	☐	☐
4. The customer can't have salt on the fries.	☐	☐
5. The customer wants cold pie.	☐	☐
6. The customer wants lots of sugar in the milkshake.	☐	☐

Listening 3

CD 1-24 ▶ Task 1

People are talking about restaurants they ate at recently. Listen and check (✓) their opinions about each restaurant.

1.

	Good	Not good
the location	☐	☑
the interior	☐	☐
the menu	☐	☐
the service	☐	☐
the prices	☐	☐

2.

	Good	Not good
the location	☐	☐
the interior	☐	☐
the menu	☐	☐
the food	☐	☐
the prices	☐	☐

3.

	Good	Not good
the location	☐	☐
the interior	☐	☐
the menu	☐	☐
the food	☐	☐
the prices	☐	☐

4.

	Good	Not good
the location	☐	☐
the interior	☐	☐
the menu	☐	☐
the food	☐	☐
the prices	☐	☐

CD 1-24 ▶ Task 2

Listen again. Did each person leave a good tip? Check (✓) the correct answer.

1. ☐ yes ☑ no
2. ☐ yes ☐ no
3. ☐ yes ☐ no
4. ☐ yes ☐ no

Making plans

Pronunciation

Reduction of *want to*

Pronunciation Help	
How we spell it	**How we say it**
want to	wanna

CD 1-25 ▶ Task 1

Listen and repeat.

1. A: What do you *want to* eat? B: I *want to* eat pizza.
2. A: Where do you *want to* go? B: I *want to* go to the Thai restaurant.

▶ Task 2

Read the sentences to a partner. Be sure to reduce *want to.*

Dictation

CD 1-26 ▶ Task 1

Listen to the conversation. Write the missing words.

A: What do you __________ __________ __________ tonight?

B: Let's go out to eat.

A: Where do you __________ __________ __________?

B: I don't know. What about you? What do you want to eat?

A: I want to go to the __________ __________.

B: I'm tired of Italian food.

A: So, what do you __________ __________ __________, then?

B: Let's order take-out Chinese!

▶ Task 2

Practice the conversation with a partner. Be sure to reduce *want to.*

Conversation

Work in pairs. Imagine you are meeting your partner for dinner.
Talk about where you want to go and what you want to eat.

UNIT 6

Gifts

Getting Ready

When do you give gifts? Check (✓) your answers and compare them with a partner. Then talk about the kinds of gifts you give for each occasion.

- ☐ birthdays
- ☐ to say "Thank you"
- ☐ weddings
- ☐ graduation
- ☐ when someone has a baby
- ☐ Mother's Day / Father's Day
- ☐ holidays
- ☐ other: ________________

CD 1-27

Listening 1

What gift does each person decide to buy? Listen and number the pictures.

A. ☐

B. ☐

C. ☐

D. ☐

E. ☐

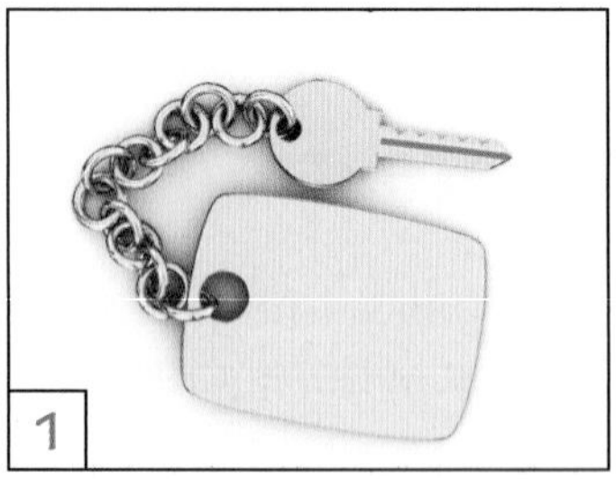
F. 1

Listening 2

CD 1-28 ▶ Task 1

People are discussing gifts in a store. Listen and check (✓) their opinions about each item.

1. Necklace

	Good	Okay	Not good
the style	☑	☐	☐
the color	☐	☐	☐
the size	☐	☐	☐

2. Shirt

	Good	Okay	Not good
the style	☐	☐	☐
the color	☐	☐	☐
the size	☐	☐	☐

3. Glasses

	Good	Okay	Not good
the style	☐	☐	☐
the color	☐	☐	☐
the size	☐	☐	☐

4. Jacket

	Good	Okay	Not good
the style	☐	☐	☐
the color	☐	☐	☐
the size	☐	☐	☐

CD 1-28 ▶ Task 2

Listen again. Do the people buy the items? Check (✓) the correct answer.

1. ☑ yes ☐ no
2. ☐ yes ☐ no
3. ☐ yes ☐ no
4. ☐ yes ☐ no

Listening 3

CD 1-29 ▶ Task 1

Salesclerks are describing gifts in a store. Listen and circle the correct information about each item.

1. The chocolates ___________.
   a. make a good souvenir
   b. are imported
   (c.) come in two kinds
2. The candles ___________.
   a. come four to a box
   b. are already gift-wrapped
   c. comes in two different sizes
3. The T-shirts ___________.
   a. are popular with teenagers
   b. come in four styles
   c. come in four sizes
4. The watches ___________.
   a. have bands made in Japan
   b. come in many sizes
   c. all look different

CD 1-29 ▶ Task 2

Listen again. What phrase completes each statement? Write the correct letter.

1. The chocolates _b_	a. are made from natural ingredients.
2. The candles ___	b. aren't right for everyone.
3. The T-shirts ___	c. fit anyone.
4. The watches ___	d. are made from cotton.

Buying a gift

Pronunciation

Syllable stress in names

Pronunciation Help

Stress the first syllable of most two-syllable names.

CD 1-30 ▶ Task 1

Listen and repeat.

1. Brándon 2. Émily 3. Dávid 4. Kátie 5. Kélly 6. María

CD 1-31 ▶ Task 2

Listen. Mark the stressed syllables in the names. Then read the sentences to a partner.

1. It's Brían's birthday next week.
2. What are you getting for Rose?
3. I'm buying a pen for Christopher.
4. Let's get Hannah some flowers.

Dictation

CD 1-32 ▶ Task 1

Listen to the conversation. Write the missing names.

A: I'm going shopping. Do you want to come with me?

B: Yes. I have to buy birthday presents for the twins, __________ and __________.

A: Oh, that reminds me! We have to get some graduation presents.

B: Right. We need something for __________.

A: And __________ is graduating, too. We need a present for him.

B: Okay. And as long as we're out, why don't we get the wedding present?

A: You mean for __________ and __________? Good idea!

▶ Task 2

Practice the conversation with a partner. Be sure to stress the names correctly.

Conversation

Work in pairs. Make a list of five of your friends.
Talk to your partner about buying a gift for each one.

UNIT 7 Air Travel

Getting Ready

Match each item in the picture with the correct word. Compare answers with a partner.

1. "No Smoking" sign h
2. customs form ___
3. headphones ___
4. seat belt ___
5. aisle seat ___
6. window seat ___
7. safety instruction card ___
8. overhead compartment ___

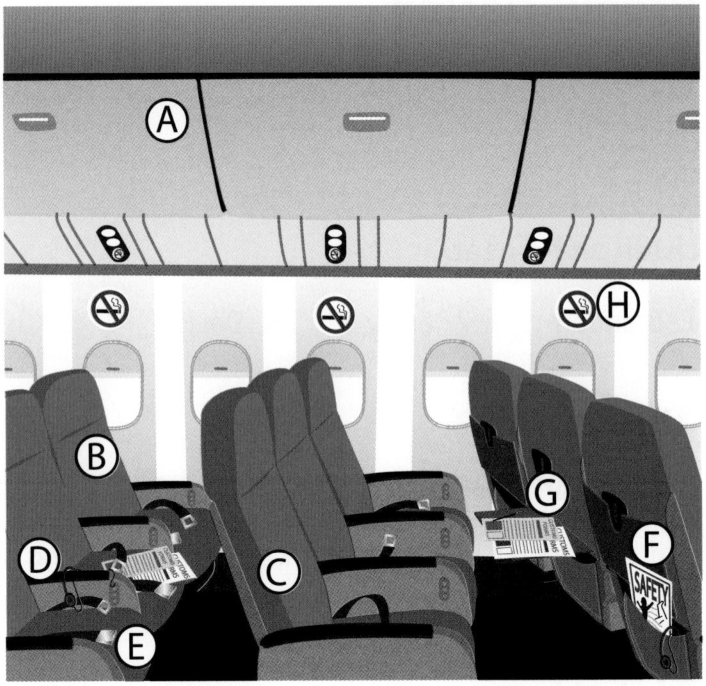

CD 1-33 Listening 1

A flight attendant is giving instructions. Listen and number the pictures.

A.

B.

C.

D.

E.

F.

Listening 2

CD 1-34 ▶ Task 1

Passengers are discussing a problem with a flight attendant. Listen and circle the correct answer.

1. a. The seat is uncomfortable.
   b. The seat is too close to the TV screen.
   (c.) The seat is too far away from the TV screen.

2. a. There's nothing in the seat pocket.
   b. There's no safety instruction card in the seat pocket.
   c. There isn't a magazine in the seat pocket.

3. a. There's no sound coming through the headphones.
   b. The sound from the headphones isn't clear.
   c. The passenger didn't get headphones.

4. a. Two passengers have the same seat number.
   b. The passenger should be in a different seat.
   c. The passenger wants to move to a window seat.

CD 1-34 ▶ Task 2

Listen again. Will the flight attendant help each passenger now or later? Check (✓) the correct answer.

1. ☐ now	2. ☐ now	3. ☐ now	4. ☐ now
☑ later	☐ later	☐ later	☐ later

Listening 3

CD 1-35 ▶ Task 1

People are talking about flights. Listen and check (✓) their opinions about each flight.

	Good	Okay	Not good
1. the airport	☐	☐	☑
the flight	☐	☐	☐
the food	☐	☐	☐
the service	☐	☐	☐
2. the airport	☐	☐	☐
the flight	☐	☐	☐
the food	☐	☐	☐
the service	☐	☐	☐
3. the airport	☐	☐	☐
the flight	☐	☐	☐
the food	☐	☐	☐
the service	☐	☐	☐
4. the airport	☐	☐	☐
the flight	☐	☐	☐
the food	☐	☐	☐
the service	☐	☐	☐

CD 1-35 ▶ Task 2

Listen again. What phrase completes each statement? Write the correct letter.

1. Next time, she won't _d_
2. Next time, he'll ____
3. Next time, she'll ____
4. Next time, he won't ____

a. try a different airline.
b. fly if the weather looks bad.
c. get a seat near the front of the plane.
d. travel during spring break.

Conversation Corner ▶ Preparing for takeoff

Pronunciation

Reduction of *could you* and *would you*

Pronunciation Help	
How we spell it	**How we say it**
Could you	Couldja
Would you	Wouldja

CD 1-36 ▶ Task 1

Listen and repeat.

1. *Could you* put your seat back up, please?
2. *Could you* fill out the form?
3. *Would you* bring me a new one?
4. *Would you* give me a hand?

▶ Task 2

Read the questions to a partner. Be sure to reduce *could you* and *would you.*

Dictation

CD 1-37 ▶ Task 1

Listen to the conversation. Write the missing words.

A: Excuse me, __________ __________ __________ that bag in the overhead compartment?

B: I'm afraid it's a bit heavy. Would you help me?

A: Sure. __________ __________ __________.

B: Thanks.

A: Oh, and we're taking off soon. __________ __________ turn off your cell phone, please?
And __________ __________ __________ your seat back forward, too?

B: No problem. Thanks for your help.

▶ Task 2

Practice the conversation with a partner. Be sure to reduce *could you* and *would you.*

Conversation

Work in pairs. Think about three things you could ask for on an airplane. Imagine your partner is a flight attendant. Ask for the things on your list. Then switch roles.

UNIT 8 Mishaps

Getting Ready

A mishap is a small accident. Match each mishap on the left with the solution on the right. Have any of these mishaps happened to you? Compare answers with a partner.

Mishap	Solution
1. You spill something on your clothes. _g_	**a.** call a tow truck
2. Your phone falls in a puddle. ___	**b.** apologize and reschedule
3. You get lost going to an appointment. ___	**c.** call a locksmith
4. You break a friend's vase. ___	**d.** call for directions
5. Your sink drain gets clogged. ___	**e.** offer to buy a new one
6. You get locked out of the house. ___	**f.** go to the store and exchange it
7. Your car won't start. ___	**g.** go to the drycleaner
8. You forgot about an appointment. ___	**h.** call a plumber

CD 1-38 Listening 1

People are talking about mishaps. Listen and number the pictures.

A. 

B. 

C. 
1

D. 

E. 

F. 

Listening 2

CD 1-39 ▶ Task 1

People are discussing mishaps.
Listen and circle the correct answer.

1. a. He spilled tomato sauce on the floor.
   (b.) He spilled tomato sauce on the rug.
2. a. He broke a teapot.
   b. He spilled tea on her clothes.
3. a. He has an ink stain on his shirt.
   b. He has a food stain on his shirt.
4. a. She lost her jacket.
   b. She spilled coffee on her jacket.
5. a. He lost his keys.
   b. He lost his wallet.
6. a. There's something wrong with the car.
   b. They're lost.

CD 1-39 ▶ Task 2

Listen again. Are these statements true or false?
Check (✓) the correct answer.

	True	False
1. The woman suggests pouring water on the stain.	☐	☑
2. The woman doesn't think an apology is a good solution.	☐	☐
3. The man doesn't agree with the woman's solution.	☐	☐
4. The woman is going to buy a new jacket.	☐	☐
5. The man is going to call a locksmith.	☐	☐
6. The man is going to call the restaurant for directions.	☐	☐

Listening 3

CD 1-40 ▶ Task 1

Four people are describing mishaps.
Listen and check (✓) the correct information.

1. Katie		
What is the mishap?	☐ She missed the bus.	☑ She dropped her cell phone.
When did it happen?	☐ this morning	☐ this afternoon
What was the solution?	☐ get a new battery	☐ dry it out
Did it work?	☐ yes	☐ no

2. Joe		
What is the mishap?	☐ He lost his keys.	☐ He lost his phone.
When did it happen?	☐ last night	☐ at lunchtime
What was the solution?	☐ go back to the store	☐ call the manager
Did it work?	☐ yes	☐ no

3. Hannah		
What is the mishap?	☐ She spilled coffee.	☐ She broke a picture.
When did it happen?	☐ this morning	☐ at the end of the day
What was the solution?	☐ soda	☐ a rug cleaner
Did it work?	☐ yes	☐ no

4. Eric		
What is the mishap?	☐ He got ink on his shirt.	☐ He got food on his shirt.
When did it happen?	☐ last week	☐ yesterday
What was the solution?	☐ take it to the drycleaner	☐ pour soda on it
Did it work?	☐ yes	☐ no

CD 1-40 ▶ Task 2

Listen again. What phrase completes each statement? Write the correct letter.

1. Katie _b_

2. Joe's manager ___

3. Hannah ___

4. Eric ___

a. charges a fee to unlock a door.

b. was running to catch the bus.

c. called his friend for a solution.

d. knocked some things off her boss's desk.

Describing a mishap

Pronunciation

Reduction of *did you*

Pronunciation Help	
How we spell it	**How we say it**
Did you	Didja

CD 1-41 ▶ Task 1

Listen and repeat.

1. *Did you* call a plumber?
2. *Did you* try pouring plain soda on it?
3. *Did you* offer to replace it?
4. *Did you* call a locksmith?
5. *Did you* take it to the dry cleaners?
6. *Did you* buy a new one?

▶ Task 2

Read the questions to a partner. Be sure to reduce *did you.*

Dictation

CD 1-42 ▶ Task 1

Listen to the conversation. Write the missing words.

A: I heard you had a terrible __________ __________. What happened?

B: I slipped on the steps. I dropped my phone and my cup of coffee!

A: Wow! __________ __________ __________ your phone?

B: Yes, but I got a new one.

A: What happened to the coffee? __________ __________ __________ it?

B: Yes. Now I have a stain on my new pants.

A: Did you take them to the dry cleaners?

B: Yes. I hope __________ __________ comes out!

▶ Task 2

Practice the conversation with a partner. Be sure to reduce *did you.*

Conversation

Work in pairs. Think of two more mishaps. Think of possible solutions for each one. Then take turns describing the mishaps and giving possible solutions.

TACTICS FOR TESTING
PAGE 100

UNIT 9 Jobs

Getting Ready

What will you think about when you look for a job?
Check (✓) your answers and compare them with a partner.

	Very important	Important	Not important
salary	☐	☐	☐
working hours	☐	☐	☐
vacations	☐	☐	☐
commuting time	☐	☐	☐
interesting work	☐	☐	☐
colleagues	☐	☐	☐
job security	☐	☐	☐
other: ________	☐	☐	☐

CD 2-2)))
Listening 1

People are talking about their jobs. Listen and number the pictures.

A. ☐

B. 1

C. ☐

D. ☐

E. ☐

F. ☐

Listening 2

CD 2-3 ▶ Task 1

What job does each person have? Listen and circle the correct answer.

1. (a.) baker
   b. manager
2. a. manager
   b. bellhop
3. a. TV producer
   b. chauffeur
4. a. technician
   b. administrative assistant
5. a. reporter
   b. photographer
6. a. cashier
   b. server

CD 2-3 ▶ Task 2

Listen again. Circle the correct answer.

1. She ___________.
   (a.) does not have a lot of experience
   b. has been working there awhile
   c. works at a theater
2. He ___________.
   a. works in the manager's office
   b. meets interesting people
   c. hates the work
3. He ___________.
   a. sees the TV producer every day
   b. helps with movie productions
   c. doesn't know how to drive
4. She ___________.
   a. thinks the salary is good
   b. is looking for another job
   c. likes her co-workers
5. He ___________.
   a. works for a magazine
   b. writes about sports news
   c. isn't famous
6. She ___________.
   a. works there only part time
   b. is a cashier
   c. doesn't work anymore

Listening 3

CD 2-4 ▶ Task 1

People are talking about their jobs. Which statement is true? Listen and circle the correct answer.

1. He __________.
   a. does all of his work on the telephone
   (b.) spends a lot of time talking to people
   c. has worked there a short time
   d. is looking for a new job

2. She __________.
   a. has a boss
   b. works for a large company
   c. has two big clients
   d. needs more work

3. He __________.
   a. has a new restaurant
   b. is very busy on the weekends
   c. has very little to do
   d. often does the cooking

4. She __________.
   a. likes meeting people
   b. doesn't really like traveling
   c. never has a break during a flight
   d. doesn't like the money

CD 2-4 ▶ Task 2

Listen again. Circle the word that each person uses to describe his or her job.

1. a. hard
   (b.) quiet
   c. interesting
   d. boring

2. a. creative
   b. boring
   c. easy
   d. unsuccessful

3. a. easy
   b. relaxing
   c. lonely
   d. tough

4. a. difficult
   b. easy
   c. tough
   d. well-paid

Describing jobs

Pronunciation

Intonation of yes/no questions

Pronunciation Help

Use rising intonation for yes/no questions.

CD 2-5 ▶ **Task 1**

Listen and repeat.

1. Do you like it there? Is it fun?
2. Do you enjoy teaching? Is it interesting?
3. Do you work in an office? Is it a full-time job?

▶ **Task 2**

Read the questions to a partner. Be sure to use the correct intonation.

Dictation

CD 2-6 ▶ **Task 1**

Listen to the conversation. Write the missing words.

A: So, what do __________ __________?

B: I'm a flight attendant.

A: That sounds interesting. Do you __________ __________ a lot?

B: Yes. I've been to over 30 countries. __________ __________ __________? What do you do?

A: I am a manager in a restaurant.

B: Do you work on __________ __________?

A: No. I travel on weekends. It's a great job!

▶ **Task 2**

Practice the conversation with a partner. Be sure to use the correct intonation.

Conversation

Work in pairs. Think of one good job and one bad job. Imagine you have one of these jobs. Take turns asking and answering questions about it. Try to guess what your partner's job is.

UNIT 10

Keeping Fit

Getting Ready

What do you do to keep fit? Match each goal on the left with the correct suggestion on the right. Compare your answers with a partner.

1. have a healthier diet c
2. tighten stomach muscles ___
3. put on weight ___
4. swim regularly ___
5. get some outdoor exercise ___

a. do lots of sit-ups
b. join a health club with a pool
c. eat less meat and more vegetables
d. lift weights every other day
e. take up jogging

CD 2-7

Listening 1

People are talking about New Year's resolutions. What is each person going to do? Listen and circle the correct answer.

1. (a.) do more exercise
   b. put on weight
2. a. learn to swim
   b. give up smoking
3. a. do more walking
   b. take up jogging
4. a. join a gym
   b. put on weight
5. a. eat less meat
   b. lose some weight
6. a. take up jogging
   b. start doing sit-ups

Listening 2

CD 2-8 ▶ Task 1

Which kind of exercise does each person prefer now? Listen and check (✓) the correct picture.

1.

a. b.

2.

a. b.

3.

a. b.

4.

a. b.

5.

a. b.

6.

a. b.

CD 2-8 ▶ Task 2

Listen again. Circle the reason each person likes the kind of exercise he or she does now.

1. **a.** It's not fun.
   (b.) It's a good place to meet people.

2. **a.** He does it indoors.
   b. He listens to the ocean as he does it.

3. **a.** It's fun.
   b. It's not easy to find a place to play.

4. **a.** It's easy to do it.
   b. She can do it almost anywhere.

5. **a.** It took a short time to learn.
   b. There are many places to ride his bike.

6. **a.** It's cheap to do.
   b. It's not as easy as it looks.

Listening 3

CD 2-9 ▶ Task 1

People are talking about exercise. Listen and check (✓) the activities they do or do not do now.

	Does	Doesn't do
1. Brandon		
a. swimming	☐	☑
b. jogging	☐	☐
c. bicycling	☐	☐
2. Alicia		
a. jogging	☐	☐
b. aerobics	☐	☐
c. weightlifting	☐	☐
3. Ian		
a. tennis	☐	☐
b. golf	☐	☐
c. weightlifting	☐	☐
4. Katie		
a. weightlifting	☐	☐
b. swimming	☐	☐
c. jogging	☐	☐

CD 2-9 ▶ Task 2

Listen again. What sport does each person want to try? Write the correct letter.

1. Brandon _b_ — **a.** swimming

2. Alicia ___ — **b.** tennis

3. Ian ___ — **c.** biking

4. Katie ___ — **d.** golf

Conversation Corner ▸ Asking about past actions

Pronunciation

Reduction of *used to* and *use to*

Pronunciation Help	
How we spell it	**How we say it**
used to	useta
use to	useta

CD 2-10 ▶ Task 1

Listen and repeat.

1. I *used to* lift weights.
2. I *didn't use to* exercise.
3. She *used to* play tennis.
4. He *didn't use to* eat right.
5. We *used to* take walks.
6. They *didn't use to* run.

▶ Task 2

Read the sentences to a partner. Be sure to reduce *used to* and *use to.*

Dictation

CD 2-11 ▶ Task 1

Listen to the conversation. Write the missing words.

A: What did you do in the past that you don't do now?

B: Well, I didn't __________ __________ workout very much.

A: So what do you do now?

B: Now, I run every day in the park. I used to __________ __________, but now I love it!

A: I __________ __________ __________ weights and use the machines at the gym.

B: And now?

A: Now I ride my bike a lot. I didn't __________ __________ __________ outdoors, but now I really enjoy it.

▶ Task 2

Practice the conversation with a partner. Be sure to reduce *used to* and *use to.*

Conversation

Work in pairs. Think about something you do now that you didn't use to do. Then tell your partner about it.

UNIT 11

Invitations

Getting Ready

Do people use these responses to accept or refuse an invitation? Check (✓) your answers and compare them with a partner.

	Accept	Refuse
1. Sorry, I'd love to, but I have other plans.	☐	☑
2. Thanks. I'd love to.	☐	☐
3. That sounds great. Thanks.	☐	☐
4. Sorry, I don't think I can.	☐	☐
5. Maybe some other time.	☐	☐
6. Sure. That sounds great.	☐	☐
7. I'd love to, but . . .	☐	☐

CD 2-12

Listening 1

What is each invitation for? Listen and circle the correct answer.

1. **a.** go to see a movie
   (b.) go for a snack
2. **a.** go to the health club
   b. go to the beach
3. **a.** see a movie
   b. rent a DVD
4. **a.** go somewhere before class
   b. go to a cafe
5. **a.** come over for dinner
   b. go to a restaurant
6. **a.** rent a DVD
   b. go to the movies

Listening 2

CD 2-13 ▶ Task 1

Does each person accept or refuse the invitation? Listen and circle the correct answer.

1. a. accept
   (b.) refuse
2. a. accept
   b. refuse
3. a. accept
   b. refuse
4. a. accept
   b. refuse
5. a. accept
   b. refuse
6. a. accept
   b. refuse

CD 2-13 ▶ Task 2

Listen again. Are these statements true or false? Check (✓) the correct answer.

	True	False
1. Melanie doesn't like musicals.	☑	☐
2. Jake goes to the park often.	☐	☐
3. Sarah has stayed home every night this week.	☐	☐
4. Ben doesn't have tickets to the game.	☐	☐
5. Jen studies Spanish.	☐	☐
6. Steven only wants to see the match.	☐	☐

Listening 3

CD 2-14 ▶ Task 1

Listen to the invitations on Erin's voicemail. Are the statements true or false? Check (✓) the correct answer.

			True	False
1.	a.	The invitation is to watch a baseball game.	☐	☑
	b.	Friends from school will be there.	☐	☐
	c.	They'll go out to eat.	☐	☐
	d.	The meeting time is 9:00 p.m.	☐	☐
2.	a.	The invitation is for lunch on Saturday.	☐	☐
	b.	It's a surprise birthday party for Meg.	☐	☐
	c.	The meeting time is noon.	☐	☐
	d.	Everyone should bring a gift.	☐	☐
3.	a.	It's an invitation from her cousin.	☐	☐
	b.	The concert is on Saturday.	☐	☐
	c.	An Australian rock group is playing.	☐	☐
	d.	They'll have dinner before the concert.	☐	☐
4.	a.	The invitation is to play tennis.	☐	☐
	b.	Some friends are meeting on Sunday afternoon.	☐	☐
	c.	The meeting time is 2:00 p.m.	☐	☐
	d.	Afterwards, they'll have dinner and see a movie.	☐	☐

CD 2-14 ▶ Task 2

Listen again. Should Erin call back or will the person call her again? Circle the correct answer.

1. (**a.**) Erin should call.
b. The caller will call again.

2. **a.** Erin should call.
b. The caller will call again.

3. **a.** Erin should call.
b. The caller will call again.

4. **a.** Erin should call.
b. The caller will call again.

Giving an invitation

Pronunciation

Reduction of *Do you* and *Are you*

Pronunciation Help	
How we spell it	**How we say it**
Do you	Doya
Are you	Areya

CD 2-15 ▶ Task 1

Listen and repeat.

1. *Do you* have any plans?
2. *Do you* want to go?
3. *Do you* like tennis?
4. *Are you* sure?
5. *Are you* free?
6. *Are you* coming?

▶ Task 2

Read the questions to a partner. Be sure to reduce *Do you* and *Are you*.

Dictation

CD 2-16 ▶ Task 1

Listen to the conversation. Write the missing words.

A: Hey, Jen. ___________ ___________ ___________ this weekend?

B: Maybe. Do you have some plans?

A: Yes. ___________ ___________ ___________ pop music?

B: Sure. Why?

A: I've got tickets for the pop music festival at Reed Hall. ___________ ___________ ___________ to come with me?

B: Do you have ___________ ___________ ___________ night or Saturday night?

A: Saturday night.

B: Great! I'd love to!

▶ Task 2

Practice the conversation with a partner. Be sure to reduce *Do you* and *Are you*.

Conversation

Work in pairs. Think of an event and plan the time and date. Take turns inviting each other to the event and accepting the invitation.

UNIT 12

Campus Life

Getting Ready

Match each place with the pictures below. Compare your answers with a partner.

a. classroom **b.** library **c.** campus bookstore

d. gym **e.** cafeteria **f.** professor's office

1. e

2.

3.

4.

5.

6.

CD 2-17

Listening 1

Where is each conversation taking place? Listen and circle the correct answer.

1. **a.** campus bookstore
   (b.) cafeteria
2. **a.** library
   b. campus bookstore
3. **a.** classroom
   b. professor's office
4. **a.** cafeteria
   b. campus bookstore
5. **a.** professor's office
   b. classroom
6. **a.** classroom
   b. gym

Listening 2

CD 2-18 ▶ Task 1

People are discussing classes they are taking. Listen and number the pictures.

A.

B.

C.

D.

E.

F.

CD 2-18 ▶ Task 2

Listen again. Are the statements true or false? Listen and check (✓) the correct answer.

	True	False
1. There isn't much reading in this class.	☐	☑
2. Students do experiments in this class.	☐	☐
3. The teacher in this class is unfair.	☐	☐
4. There's a lot of homework for this class.	☐	☐
5. The professor is interesting.	☐	☐
6. This class meets in a lab.	☐	☐

Listening 3

CD 2-19 ▶ Task 1

People are talking about their schools. Listen and check (✓) their opinions about each school.

1.

	Positive	Negative
campus	☑	☐
teachers	☐	☐
schedule	☐	☐
students	☐	☐

2.

	Positive	Negative
campus	☐	☐
gym	☐	☐
teachers	☐	☐
schedule	☐	☐

3.

	Positive	Negative
classes	☐	☐
students	☐	☐
clubs	☐	☐
campus	☐	☐

4.

	Positive	Negative
teachers	☐	☐
campus	☐	☐
schedule	☐	☐
students	☐	☐

CD 2-19 ▶ Task 2

Listen again. What phrase completes each statement? Write the correct letter.

1. The teachers _c_
2. The gym ___
3. The campus ___
4. The students ___

a. is modern and looks nice.
b. are different here.
c. are not interested in teaching.
d. has an outdoor cafe.

Describing likes and dislikes

Pronunciation

Intonation of words in a series

Pronunciation Help

When listing a series, use falling intonation for the last item in a series and rising intonation for earlier items.

CD 2-20 ▶ Task 1

Listen and repeat.

1. I like the campus, the classes, and the teachers.
2. She likes the food, the people, and the sports.
3. I don't like my schedule, my teachers, or the homework.

▶ Task 2

Read the sentences to a partner. Be sure to use the correct intonation.

Dictation

CD 2-21 ▶ Task 1

Listen to the conversation. Write the missing words.

A: So, how do you like your school?

B: Well, I like some things, but I __________ __________ __________ things.

A: Such as?

B: I like the __________, the __________, and the __________. But I don't like the food, the gym, or the clubs. How about you?

A: Just the opposite! I really like the __________, the __________, and the __________.

B: What don't you like?

A: I guess I __________ __________ __________ the classes, the teachers, and the homework!

▶ Task 2

Practice the conversation with a partner. Be sure to use the correct intonation.

Conversation

Work in pairs. What do you like about your school? What don't you like about your school? Take turns talking about what you like and dislike about your school.

TACTICS FOR TESTING
PAGE 102

UNIT 13

Hobbies and Pastimes

Getting Ready

Who would most enjoy these hobbies and pastimes? Check (✓) your answers and compare them with a partner. There may be more than one answer.

	Young child	Teenager	Adult	Retired person
gardening	☐	☐	☐	☐
cooking	☐	☐	☐	☐
playing sports	☐	☐	☐	☐
hiking	☐	☐	☐	☐
collecting comic books	☐	☐	☐	☐
playing video games	☐	☐	☐	☐
surfing the Internet	☐	☐	☐	☐

CD 2-22 Listening 1

People are talking about hobbies and pastimes. Listen and number the pictures.

A. 

B. 

C. 

D. 

E. 1 

F. 

Listening 2

CD 2-23 ▶ Task 1

Which activity does each person enjoy doing now? Listen and circle the correct answer.

1. Zach
   a. playing basketball
   (b.) painting
   c. hiking

2. Erica
   a. collecting baseball cards
   b. collecting comic books
   c. gardening

3. Brian
   a. watching videos
   b. hiking
   c. playing video games

4. Evan
   a. collecting stamps
   b. collecting paintings
   c. collecting baseball cards

5. Danielle
   a. painting
   b. writing children's books
   c. reading

6. Marcus
   a. reading the newspaper
   b. playing golf
   c. reading books

CD 2-23 ▶ Task 2

Listen again. What does each speaker like best about his or her current hobby or pastime? Write the correct letter.

1. Zach _d_
2. Erica ___
3. Brian ___
4. Evan ___
5. Danielle ___
6. Marcus ___

a. the flowers
b. looking at his collection
c. creating pictures
d. using bright colors
e. looking at the blue sky
f. making great friends

Listening 3

CD 2-24 ▶ Task 1

People are talking about their interests. Listen and check (✓) two suitable hobbies for each person.

1. Steve
   - ☐ surfing the Internet
   - ☑ gardening
   - ☑ bird watching
   - ☐ hiking

2. Christine
   - ☐ music
   - ☐ bird watching
   - ☐ gardening
   - ☐ cooking

3. Joe
   - ☐ sports
   - ☐ hiking
   - ☐ music
   - ☐ surfing the Internet

4. Amy
   - ☐ hiking
   - ☐ reading
   - ☐ sports
   - ☐ surfing the Internet

CD 2-24 ▶ Task 2

Listen again. What is one activity each person likes doing? Circle the correct answer.

1. **a.** enjoying nature
   b. hiking
   c. sitting in a cafe

2. **a.** bird watching
   b. visiting the countryside
   c. getting together with friends

3. **a.** surfing the Internet
   b. exercising
   c. playing the guitar

4. **a.** learning something new
   b. going to parties
   c. working out at the gym

Talking about hobbies

Pronunciation

Syllable stress in words

Pronunciation Help

Tap your desk as you say the words. It will help you hear which syllables are stressed.

CD 2-25 ▶ Task 1

Listen and repeat.

1. báseball 2. cóoking 3. gárdening 4. réstaurants 5. híking 6. páinting

CD 2-26 ▶ Task 2

Listen. Mark the stressed syllable in the underlined words. Then read the sentences to a partner.

1. He collects <u>cómic</u> books. 2. They love <u>playing</u> golf. 3. She enjoys watching <u>videos</u>.

Dictation

CD 2-27 ▶ Task 1

Listen to the conversation. Write the missing words.

A: What do you do in your free time, Lara?

B: I used to enjoy ________, but now I like ________ and ________.

A: Oh, not me! I enjoy collecting things. I collect ________ cards.

B: Do you do anything else?

A: Yes, I really enjoy ________ the Internet and listening to ________.

B: Do you play any sports?

A: I go ________ and ________ in the winter. How about you?

B: I like summer sports. I enjoy ________ and ________.

▶ Task 2

Practice the conversation with a partner. Be sure to stress the correct syllable in the missing words.

Conversation

Work in pairs. Think about your own hobbies and pastimes.
Ask and answer questions about them with your partner.

UNIT 14 Shopping Problems

Getting Ready

Have you ever had these problems? Check (✓) your answers and compare them with a partner.

You bought something that ___________.

- ☐ shrank when you washed it
- ☐ had a missing part
- ☐ was the wrong size
- ☐ didn't work
- ☐ changed color when you washed it
- ☐ was damaged
- ☐ was poorly made
- ☐ other: ________________

CD 2-28 Listening 1

Which item did each person receive? Listen and check (✓) the correct picture.

1.

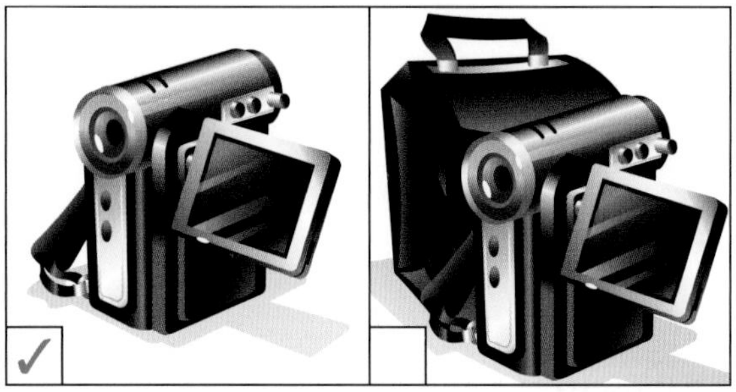

a. b.

2.

a. b.

3.

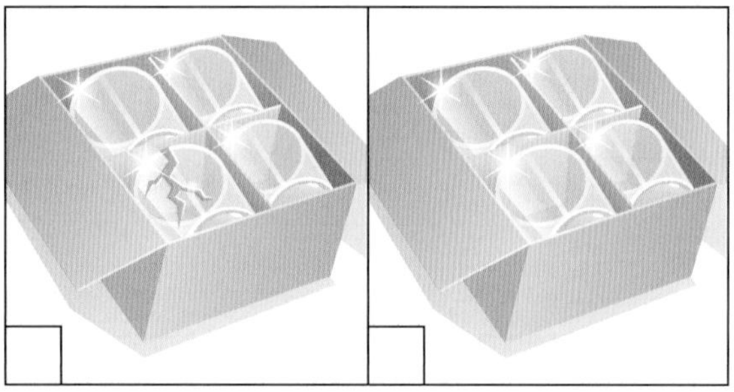

a. b.

4.

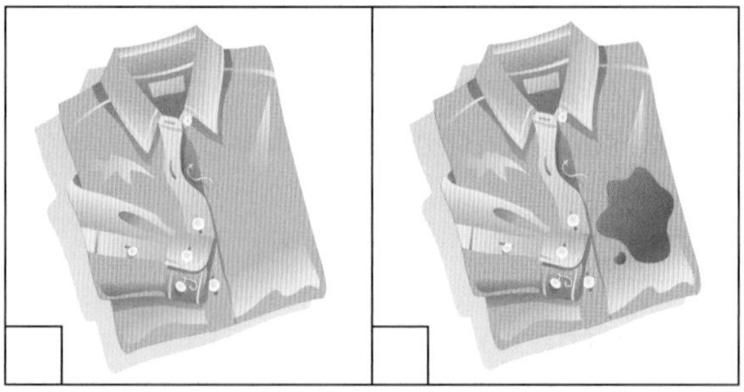

a. b.

Listening 2

CD 2-29 ▶ Task 1

Customers are describing a problem. Listen and circle the correct answer.

1. (a.) She needs a bigger size.
   b. She needs a smaller size.

2. a. The shoes are too small.
   b. The shoes are damaged.

3. a. The lock is missing.
   b. The lock isn't working.

4. a. The band is too big.
   b. The band is broken.

5. a. The shirt has shrunk.
   b. The buttons have come off the shirt.

6. a. The back doesn't close.
   b. The shutter is broken.

CD 2-29 ▶ Task 2

Listen again. Are these statements true or false?
Check (✓) the correct answer.

	True	False
1. The clerk asks the customer to come back tomorrow.	☐	☑
2. The clerk asks for the receipt.	☐	☐
3. The customer has to bring the briefcase back in a few days.	☐	☐
4. The customer should call the clerk by tonight.	☐	☐
5. The clerk asks the customer to fill out a form.	☐	☐
6. The customer needs to show the clerk the guarantee.	☐	☐

Listening 3

CD 2-30 ▶ Task 1

People are talking about shopping. Listen and circle the correct information about each person.

1. a. She enjoyed going to the store.
   (b.) There were good bargains.
   c. She bought many things.

2. a. He didn't like the clothes he bought.
   b. He didn't buy much.
   c. Most of the things he bought were good.

3. a. The camera cost nearly $250.
   b. The camera doesn't work well.
   c. The camera cost more at an online store.

4. a. She thought the prices were reasonable.
   b. She bargained when she bought them.
   c. Her friend got things for a higher price.

CD 2-30 ▶ Task 2

Listen again. What phrase completes each statement? Write the correct letter.

1. Next time, she won't _b_
2. Next time, he'll save his money and ___
3. Next time, he'll spend more time ___
4. Next time, she'll be sure to ___

a. comparing prices before buying something.
b. go shopping during a big sale.
c. bargain.
d. wait for the sales at home.

Returning an item

Pronunciation

Reduction of *need to* and *like to*

Pronunciation Help	
How we spell it	**How we say it**
need to	needta
like to	liketa

CD 2-31 ▶ Task 1

Listen and repeat.

1. I *need to* return this.
2. You *need to* show me the guarantee.
3. He *needs to* get another size.
4. I'd *like to* exchange these shoes.
5. She'd *like to* get a refund.
6. We'd *like to* get another one.

▶ Task 2

Read the sentences to a partner. Be sure to reduce *need to* and *like to.*

Dictation

CD 2-32 ▶ Task 1

Listen to the conversation. Write the missing words.

A: Can I help you?

B: Yes, I'd __________ __________ __________ this shirt. I need to get a larger one.

A: No problem.

B: And the color is wrong. I'd like to find a __________ __________.

A: That's fine. Oh, and do you have your receipt?

B: Uh-oh, I think I forgot it. I __________ __________ go home and get it.

A: Yes, I __________ __________ __________ your receipt.

B: Okay, I'll be right back.

▶ Task 2

Practice the conversation with a partner. Be sure to reduce *need to* and *like to.*

Conversation

Work in pairs. Think of something you recently bought. Imagine it has a problem. Take turns being a salesperson and a customer, and return the item to the store.

UNIT 15 Hotel Services

Getting Ready

Which numbers in a hotel do you call for the following services?
Write the numbers next to the services. Compare answers with a partner.

1. To order a meal in your room, dial 15.
2. To get clothes dry cleaned, dial ___.
3. To get help carrying your bags, dial ___.
4. To get your room cleaned, dial ___.
5. To get theater tickets, dial ___.
6. To check if you have received mail, dial ___.

CD 2-33

Listening 1

People are making calls from their hotel rooms. Who is each person calling?
Listen and circle the correct answer.

1. (a.) laundry
   b. room service
2. a. concierge
   b. bell captain
3. a. housekeeping
   b. room service
4. a. bell captain
   b. laundry
5. a. front desk
   b. room service
6. a. concierge
   b. housekeeping

Vocabulary Worksheet

Listening 2

CD 2-34 ▶ Task 1

People are talking to a hotel receptionist. What does each person want to do? Listen and circle the correct answer.

1. a. leave a message
   (b.) check for packages
   c. pick up mail

2. a. move to a bigger room
   b. move to a quieter room
   c. move to a smoking room

3. a. arrange for a taxi for the morning
   b. arrange for a taxi for tonight
   c. learn to set the alarm clock

4. a. drive to a restaurant
   b. eat something without meat
   c. eat in the restaurant

CD 2-34 ▶ Task 2

Listen again. Are these statements true or false? Check (✓) the correct answer.

	True	False
1. The guest has no package.	☑	☐
2. The guest hates the smell of smoke.	☐	☐
3. The guest can get ready in 30 minutes.	☐	☐
4. The guest can't order lasagna without meat.	☐	☐

Listening 3

CD 2-35 ▶ Task 1

People are talking about the hotels they are staying in. Listen and check (✓) their opinions about each hotel.

1.

	Good	Not Good
the restaurant	☐	☑
the service	☐	☐
the room	☐	☐
the rates	☐	☐

2.

	Good	Not Good
the restaurant	☐	☐
the service	☐	☐
the room	☐	☐
the rates	☐	☐

3.

	Good	Not Good
the restaurant	☐	☐
the service	☐	☐
the room	☐	☐
the rates	☐	☐

4.

	Good	Not Good
the restaurant	☐	☐
the service	☐	☐
the room	☐	☐
the rates	☐	☐

CD 2-35 ▶ Task 2

Listen again. What phrase completes each statement? Write the correct letter.

1. The hotel should have one restaurant that's __a__
2. The hotel should buy ___
3. The hotel should get ___
4. The hotel should have at least one ___

a. just for adults.
b. a new manager.
c. cheap, casual restaurant.
d. softer mattresses.

Conversation Corner ▸ Asking for help

Pronunciation

Reduction of the vowel sound in *can*

Pronunciation Help	
How we spell it	**How we say it**
can	kən
can't	kænt

CD 2-36 ▶ **Task 1**

Listen and repeat.

1. *Can* I help you?
2. *Can* I get them tonight?
3. You *can* leave them here.
4. I *can't* open the window.
5. I *can't* find my key.
6. I *can't* connect to the Internet.

▶ **Task 2**

Read the sentences to a partner. Be sure to reduce the vowel sound in *can.*

Dictation

CD 2-37 ▶ **Task 1**

Listen to the conversation. Write the missing words.

A: __________ __________ help you?

B: Yes. I can't open the window in my room. __________ __________ get some help?

A: Certainly. Is there anything else?

B: Yes. I __________ __________ the air conditioner off.

A: We can help with that. Is there anything else I can do?

B: Yes. I __________ __________ to the Internet.

A: You need a password. I __________ __________ __________ up with it.

B: Thank you very much!

▶ **Task 2**

Practice the conversation with a partner. Be sure to reduce the vowel sound in *can.*

Conversation

Work in pairs. Imagine you are staying in a hotel. Ask your partner for something you need or something you need help with. Take turns being the guest and receptionist.

UNIT 16

Movies

Getting Ready

Look at the pictures. What kind of movie does each one show?

Match each kind of movie on the left with the best description on the right. Compare answers with a partner.

1. romance _b_
2. western ___
3. horror ___
4. action ___
5. science fiction ___
6. comedy ___

a. A movie about events that take place in the future or in other parts of the universe.
b. A movie that tells a love story.
c. A movie about life in the west of the United States in the nineteenth century.
d. A movie that tries to scare the audience.
e. A movie that tries to make people laugh.
f. A movie with a fast-moving story that is full of danger and excitement.

CD 2-38

Listening 1

What kind of movie does each person describe? Listen and circle the correct answer.

1. a. science fiction
   (b.) action
2. a. action
   b. comedy
3. a. horror
   b. western
4. a. science fiction
   b. comedy
5. a. romance
   b. western
6. a. action
   b. science fiction

Listening 2

CD 2-39 ▶ Task 1

People are looking at information about movies on a website. What type of movie is it? Listen and write the correct letter.

a. western b. comedy c. horror d. action e. science fiction f. romance

1. CINEMA 1

title: Hit Harder: The Final Conflict

type: d

2. CINEMA 2

title: Party Animal

type: ___

3. CINEMA 3

title: Dreams

type: ___

4. CINEMA 4

title: Cowboy's Run

type: ___

5. CINEMA 5

title: Space Children

type: ___

6. CINEMA 6

title: Monster Party

type: ___

CD 2-39 ▶ Task 2

Listen again. Write the show times.

Cinema 1 2:30, 4:45, 7:30, 10:00

Cinema 2 ___

Cinema 3 ___

Cinema 4 ___

Cinema 5 ___

Cinema 6 ___

Listening 3

CD 2-40 ▶ Task 1

People are talking about movies. What did they like or not like about each movie? Listen and check (✓) the correct answers.

1.

	Liked	Didn't like
the story	☐	☑
the acting	☐	☐
the ending	☐	☐
the music	☐	☐

2.

	Liked	Didn't like
the story	☐	☐
the acting	☐	☐
the ending	☐	☐
the music	☐	☐

3.

	Liked	Didn't like
the story	☐	☐
the acting	☐	☐
the ending	☐	☐
the music	☐	☐

4.

	Liked	Didn't like
the story	☐	☐
the acting	☐	☐
the ending	☐	☐
the music	☐	☐

CD 2-40 ▶ Task 2

Listen again. Does each person recommend the movie or not? Check (✓) the correct answer.

1. ☐ yes ☑ no
2. ☐ yes ☐ no
3. ☐ yes ☐ no
4. ☐ yes ☐ no

Conversation Corner Talking about movies

Pronunciation

Linked sounds *s* and *z*

CD 2-41 ▶ Task 1

Listen and repeat. Notice the linked sounds.

1. What was it about?
2. What's it about?
3. It's about a wedding.
4. Who was in it?
5. Who's in it?
6. She's in a new movie.

Pronunciation Help

How we spell it	How we say it
is it	izit
was it	wazit
who's in	whozin
it's about	itsabout
what's it	whatsit
what's on	whatson

▶ Task 2

Read the sentences to a partner. Be sure to link the *s* and *z* sounds.

Dictation

CD 2-42 ▶ Task 1

Listen to the conversation. Write the missing words.

A: Hey, would you like to go to a movie tonight?

B: Yeah, I'd love to. __________ __________?

A: *Hats off to Harry* is playing at the Gateway Theater. __________ __________ a boy that gets lost, ends up in Hollywood, and becomes a big star.

B: __________ __________ it?

A: Well, besides the boy, umm, Russell Hill.

B: Oh, __________ __________ funny guy. Let's go!

▶ Task 2

Practice the conversation with a partner. Be sure to link the *s* and *z* sounds.

Conversation

Work in pairs. Think of two new movies.
Take turns inviting each other to one of the movies.
Ask what the movie is about before you accept the invitation.

TACTICS FOR TESTING
PAGE 104

UNIT 17

Fears

Getting Ready

Are you afraid of any of the things below? Check (✓) your answers and compare them with a partner.

	Yes	No
heights	☐	☐
riding roller coasters	☐	☐
spiders	☐	☐
snakes	☐	☐
mice	☐	☐
cockroaches	☐	☐
bats	☐	☐
small spaces	☐	☐
scuba diving	☐	☐
flying on airplanes	☐	☐
driving on freeways	☐	☐
other: ____________	☐	☐

CD 3-2 Listening 1

What is happening in these pictures? Listen and number the pictures.

A. ☐

B. ☐

C. 1

D. ☐

E. ☐

F. ☐

Listening 2

CD 3-3 ▶ Task 1

Look at the picture. What is she doing?

People are describing fears. Has each speaker's fear decreased over the years? Listen and check (✓) the correct answer.

1. ☑ yes ☐ no
2. ☐ yes ☐ no
3. ☐ yes ☐ no
4. ☐ yes ☐ no
5. ☐ yes ☐ no
6. ☐ yes ☐ no

CD 3-3 ▶ Task 2

Listen again. Circle the correct statement.

1. **a.** She loved going to the zoo when she was a kid.
   (b.) She was given a kitten for her birthday.
2. **a.** A snake tried to bite her while she was hiking.
   b. A snake bit her at the zoo.
3. **a.** His friend hated spiders.
   b. He studied spiders in college.
4. **a.** He learned how to swim.
   b. He went to the beach often when he was a kid.
5. **a.** His friend was in a car accident.
   b. He was in a car accident.
6. **a.** She learned to fly a plane.
   b. An airplane engineer explained how planes stay in the air.

Listening 3

CD 3-4 ▶ Task 1

People are talking about their fears. Is each statement true or false? Listen and check (✓) the correct answer.

	True	False
1. a. He has never had bad experiences in elevators.	☐	☑
b. He doesn't like the feeling of not being able to get out.	☐	☐
2. a. She is afraid of waves.	☐	☐
b. She likes pools because there are lots of people around.	☐	☐
3. a. She is afraid of cats.	☐	☐
b. She has been chased by birds.	☐	☐
4. a. He doesn't mind looking out of windows on high floors.	☐	☐
b. He doesn't like flying.	☐	☐

CD 3-4 ▶ Task 2

Listen again. What problem does the fear cause for each person? Circle the correct answer.

1. **a.** He can never use elevators.
   b. He hates using stairs.
   (c.) He has to use the elevator with someone else.

2. **a.** She can't swim in a pool.
   b. She can't swim in the ocean.
   c. She can't be in crowds.

3. **a.** She can't visit her friend with a bird.
   b. She can't visit her friend with a cat.
   c. She can't visit the beach with her friends.

4. **a.** He can't work in a tall building.
   b. He never travels.
   c. He can't do some fun things with his kids.

Pronunciation

Sentence stress

CD 3-5 ▶ Task 1

Listen and repeat.

1. Ónce, I sát next to an áirplane enginéer.
2. Whén I was a kíd, I got stúck in an élevator.
3. Áfter we were in the áir for a whíle, I félt a lot bétter.
4. Thén when I wént to cóllege, I léarned about spíders.

Pronunciation Help

Tap your desk as you say the sentences. It will help you hear which words and syllables are stressed.

▶ Task 2

Read the sentences to a partner. Be sure to stress the correct words and syllables.

Dictation

CD 3-6 ▶ Task 1

Listen to the conversation. Write the missing words.

A: Are you afraid of anything?

B: Yes. I'm afraid of elevators. Once, when I was a kid, I got stuck in __________ __________.

A: So what do you do when you have to take an elevator?

B: I try to __________ __________ __________! How about you?

A: I was afraid of insects when I was a kid.

B: How did you stop being __________ __________ insects?

A: When I was in college, I studied insects in a __________ __________. Now, I'm not afraid at all. In fact, I think __________ __________ __________!

▶ Task 2

Practice the conversation with a partner. Be sure to stress the correct words and syllables.

Conversation

Work in pairs. Think of something that you were afraid of when you were a child. Ask and answer questions about what you were afraid of. Tell your partner if you're still afraid of it now.

UNIT 18

Phone Messages

Getting Ready

Do you use your phone often? Think about the questions below. Discuss your answers with a partner.

1. How many phone calls do you make a day?
2. How many phone calls do you receive a day?
3. Who do you call most often?
4. How many text messages do you send a day?
5. How many text messages do you receive a day?
6. Who do you text most often?
7. What else do you use your cell phone for?
8. Do you prefer making phone calls or texting? Why?

CD 3-7

Listening 1

Listen to the messages on Lara's voicemail. Complete the information about each call.

1. **Important Message**

   Name of caller: David
   Telephone number: 981-2146
   Best time to call: after ______

2. **Important Message**

   Name of caller: Sarah
   Telephone number: ______
   Best time to call: between ___ and ___

3. **Important Message**

   Name of caller: Peter ______
   Telephone number: ______
   Best time to call: between ___ and ___

4. **Important Message**

   Name of caller: Linda Wong
   Telephone number: ______
   Best time to call: ______

Listening 2

CD 3-8 ▶ Task 1

Listen to these messages on Andre's voicemail. Circle the correct message.

1. **a.** Pick up the car on Tuesday morning.
   (b.) Pick up the car on Friday afternoon.
2. **a.** ABC Express will deliver a package tomorrow.
   b. ABC Express delivered a package today.
3. **a.** Susan is inviting Andre to a party on Saturday.
   b. Susan is telling Andre she will come to his party.
4. **a.** The shirt has arrived.
   b. The shirt hasn't arrived yet.
5. **a.** Kathy cannot go to dinner.
   b. Kathy can go to dinner after work.
6. **a.** Dr. Costello can give Andre a dental appointment on Thursday.
   b. Dr. Costello can give Andre a dental appointment on Tuesday.

CD 3-8 ▶ Task 2

Listen again. Does the caller want Andre to call back or will the caller phone again later? Check (✓) the correct answer.

	Andre should return the call.	The caller will telephone Andre.
1.	☑	☐
2.	☐	☐
3.	☐	☐
4.	☐	☐
5.	☐	☐
6.	☐	☐

Listening 3

CD 3-9 ▶ Task 1

Daniel is listening to messages on his voicemail at work. Is each statement true or false? Listen and check (✓) the correct answer.

		True	False
1.	a. The message is from an airline company.	☐	☑
	b. The flights are confirmed.	☐	☐
	c. Free transportation to the hotel is available.	☐	☐
	d. The driver should not be tipped.	☐	☐
2.	a. The message is from the mailroom.	☐	☐
	b. The package is waiting.	☐	☐
	c. The mailroom will deliver the package.	☐	☐
	d. He received a letter.	☐	☐
3.	a. The invitation is for dinner.	☐	☐
	b. He wants to go to a Mexican restaurant.	☐	☐
	c. He suggests a boat trip after the meal.	☐	☐
	d. He will call again later.	☐	☐
4.	a. The shirts can be picked up now.	☐	☐
	b. The store is open until 9:00 p.m.	☐	☐
	c. The cost is $29.	☐	☐
	d. You can pay by check or credit card.	☐	☐

CD 3-9 ▶ Task 2

Listen again. What is each caller's phone number? Write the answers.

1. Mary *878-1990*
2. Peter ____________
3. Mike ____________
4. Mrs. Jones ____________

Conversation Corner ▸ Saying phone numbers

Pronunciation

Intonation of phone numbers

Pronunciation Help

The number 0 in phone numbers is pronounced *oh* or zero.

CD 3-10 ▶ Task 1

Listen and repeat.

1. 415-555-6879
2. 404-619-4967
3. 555-212-6978

CD 3-11 ▶ Task 2

Listen. Mark arrows over the numbers where your voice rises and where it falls. Then read the sentences to a partner.

1. Call me at 878-858-1990.
2. I'm at 392-4592.
3. Her number is 451-760-6024.

Dictation

CD 3-12 ▶ Task 1

Listen to the conversation. Write the missing numbers.

A: Mike called today. He wants to go to the restaurant with us tonight.

B: Did he leave his number?

A: Yes. It's ____________. He also asked us to invite Lisa.

B: Did he leave her number?

A: No, but I have it memorized. It's ____________.

B: Got it. We should call the restaurant, too. I think their number is ____________.

▶ Task 2

Practice the conversation with a partner. Be sure to use the correct intonation.

Conversation

Work in pairs. Imagine you are meeting your partner for the first time.
Write down each other's phone numbers.
Then check to see if you wrote the numbers correctly.

UNIT 19

Touring a City

Getting Ready

Look at the picture. Where are the people?

What do you do when you visit a new city? Check (✓) your answers and compare them with a partner.

- ☐ visit museums
- ☐ visit churches or temples
- ☐ take a bus tour
- ☐ try local food
- ☐ go to the zoo
- ☐ buy souvenirs
- ☐ go shopping
- ☐ attend local cultural events
- ☐ other: ________________

CD 3-13 Listening 1

People are visiting a city. Where are they? Listen and number the pictures.

A. 

B. 

C. 

D. 

E. 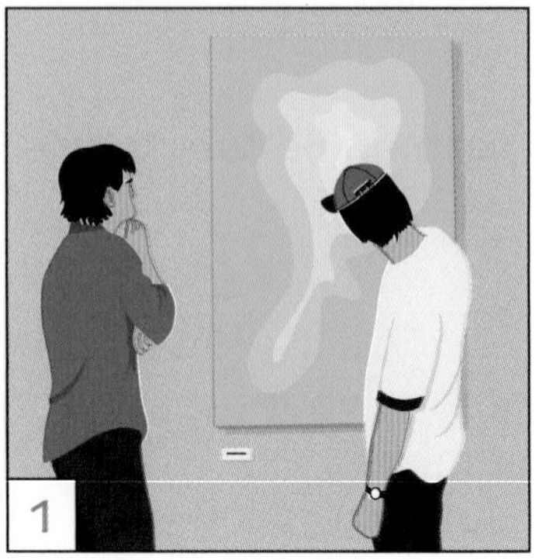

F. 

Listening 2

CD 3-14 ▶ Task 1

Tour guides are describing some of the things people will see or do on a bus tour. Listen and circle the correct answers.

1. a. take pictures of the stars' houses
   (b.) see Marilyn Monroe's house
   c. see Joe DiMaggio's house
   d. see James Dean's house
   e. see Arnold Schwarzenegger's house

2. a. go to the Empire State Building
   b. visit the Statue of Liberty
   c. take a taxi uptown
   d. have a picnic in Central Park
   e. go ice skating at Rockefeller Center

3. a. hike in the mountains
   b. visit a market
   c. eat food at the market
   d. go inside a temple
   e. touch the statues

4. a. see a cemetery
   b. go to a museum
   c. visit a famous person's grave
   d. go to the museum shop
   e. go to an open-air market

CD 3-14 ▶ Task 2

Listen again. Are these statements true or false? Check (✓) the correct answer.

	True	False
1. People can take pictures of the stars' houses.	☐	☑
2. People can buy a photo of the ice rink.	☐	☐
3. People can buy many kinds of souvenirs.	☐	☐
4. People can't take pictures of the graves.	☐	☐

Listening 3

CD 3-15 ▶ Task 1

People are talking about the tours they took. What was good or bad about each tour? Listen and check (✓) the correct answer.

1.

	Good	Not good
the itinerary	☐	☑
the guide	☐	☐
the food	☐	☐
the price	☐	☐

3.

	Good	Not good
the itinerary	☐	☐
the guide	☐	☐
the food	☐	☐
the price	☐	☐

2.

	Good	Not good
the itinerary	☐	☐
the guide	☐	☐
the food	☐	☐
the price	☐	☐

4.

	Good	Not good
the itinerary	☐	☐
the guide	☐	☐
the food	☐	☐
the price	☐	☐

CD 3-15 ▶ Task 2

Listen again. Would each person recommend the tour? Check (✓) the correct answer.

1. ☐ yes
☑ no

2. ☐ yes
☐ no

3. ☐ yes
☐ no

4. ☐ yes
☐ no

Describing a city

Pronunciation

Reduction of –*est* in superlatives

Pronunciation Help	
How we spell it	**How we say it**
biggest	biggus
oldest	oldus
tallest	tallus

CD 3-16 ▶ **Task 1**

Listen and repeat.

1. It's the *tallest* building in New York City.
2. Mt. Whitney is the *highest* mountain in California.
3. This is the *biggest* shopping mall in the world.
4. It's the *largest* city in Latin America.
5. It's the *shortest* train track.
6. This is the *oldest* theater in the city.

▶ **Task 2**

Read the sentences to a partner. Be sure to reduce –*est* in the superlatives.

Dictation

CD 3-17 ▶ **Task 1**

Listen to the conversation. Write the missing words.

A: What did you see on your tour?

B: We first saw the Grant House. It's __________ __________ building in the city.

A: Nice. What else did you see?

B: Then we visited the park. It's one of the __________ __________ __________ in the country. After that, we went to the top of the mountain.

A: Oh, I bet the view was great. Isn't that one of the __________ __________ in the state?

B: Yes. Actually, it's the __________ __________ in the country. The view __________ __________.

▶ **Task 2**

Practice the conversation with a partner. Be sure to reduce –*est* in the superlatives.

Conversation

Work in pairs. Imagine you and your partner are going to take a visitor on a tour of your town or city. Talk about what your visitor should see and why.

UNIT 20 Airports

Getting Ready

Match each activity on the left with the correct place on the right. Compare answers with a partner.

1. freshen up after a flight _d_
2. board a flight ___
3. meet a friend arriving on a flight ___
4. get flight information ___
5. change money ___
6. pick up suitcases after a flight ___
7. buy a magazine ___
8. take a bus to a different terminal ___

a. arrivals area
b. baggage claim area
c. newsstand
d. restroom
e. shuttle bus stop
f. departure gate
g. currency exchange
h. arrival and departure board

CD 3-18 Listening 1

Where do these people want to go? Listen and check (✓) the correct picture.

1.

a.

b. ✓

2.

a.

b.

3.

a.

b.

4.

a.

b.

Listening 2

CD 3-19 ▶ Task 1

What are these people talking about? Listen and circle the correct answer.

1. (a.) directions
   b. flight insurance
   c. flight information

2. a. ticketing information
   b. a flight departure time
   c. a flight arrival time

3. a. transportation to the hotel
   b. hotel prices
   c. car rentals

4. a. customs and immigration
   b. shopping
   c. ATM machines

CD 3-19 ▶ Task 2

Listen again. Are these statements true or false? Check (✓) the correct answer.

	True	False
1. a. He needs to find Terminal B.	☑	☐
b. The bus leaves in twenty minutes.	☐	☐
c. He doesn't need to buy a ticket.	☐	☐
2. a. The clerk doesn't help the man.	☐	☐
b. The flight arrival time will appear later.	☐	☐
c. The man should check the monitor in 50 minutes.	☐	☐
3. a. There are maps on Level 1.	☐	☐
b. She plans to drive to the hotel.	☐	☐
c. The hotel is near the airport.	☐	☐
4. a. There aren't a lot of stores to choose from.	☐	☐
b. She doesn't have to go through customs and immigration first.	☐	☐
c. She can't use credit cards.	☐	☐

Listening 3

CD 3-20 ▶ Task 1

People are talking about airports in different cities. Listen and check (✓) the correct answers.

1.

	Good	Not good
the location	☑	☐
the transportation	☐	☐
the facilities	☐	☐
the check-in	☐	☐

2.

	Good	Not good
the location	☐	☐
the transportation	☐	☐
the facilities	☐	☐
the check-in	☐	☐

3.

	Good	Not good
the location	☐	☐
the transportation	☐	☐
the facilities	☐	☐
the check-in	☐	☐

4.

	Good	Not good
the location	☐	☐
the transportation	☐	☐
the facilities	☐	☐
the check-in	☐	☐

CD 3-20 ▶ Task 2

Listen again. What phrase completes each statement? Write the correct letter.

1. The airport should put in _b_
2. The airport needs to add ___
3. There should be ___
4. The city needs to build ___

a. some more check-in counters.
b. some stores and cafes.
c. a new airport closer to the city.
d. a bus service into town.

Conversation Corner ▸ Asking directions

Pronunciation

Plural –*s* endings

CD 3-21 ▶ **Task 1**

Listen and repeat.

1. The flights are late.
2. The next plane leaves in 30 minutes.
3. The restrooms are down the stairs.
4. There are a lot of good places to eat.

Pronunciation Help

Sounds like /s/	Sounds like /z/	Sounds like /iz/
flights	bags	buses
minutes	stairs	places
tickets	taxis	suitcases

▶ **Task 2**

Read the sentences to a partner. Be sure to pronounce the –*s* endings correctly.

Dictation

CD 3-22 ▶ **Task 1**

Listen to the conversation. Write the missing words.

A: Excuse me, where are __________ __________?

B: Your bags are in the baggage claim area, on carousel 3.

A: Thanks. Oh, and are there __________ __________ to eat near the baggage claim area?

B: Yes. There are two cafes and a couple of __________.

A: Great. How do we get into the city?

B: There are __________ __________ __________ just outside, after you leave the baggage area.

A: Thank you so much!

▶ **Task 2**

Practice the conversation with a partner. Be sure to pronounce the –*s* endings correctly.

Conversation

Work in pairs. Make a list of three places you can ask directions to in an airport. Then take turns asking for and giving directions for the places on your list.

TACTICS FOR TESTING
PAGE 106

UNIT 21

Hotels

Getting Ready

Look at the pictures. What are these items?

What do you usually do when you check into a hotel? Check (✓) your answers and compare them with a partner.

- ☐ show some identification
- ☐ give your credit card number
- ☐ pay for the room in advance
- ☐ pay a deposit
- ☐ show a letter from your company or school
- ☐ fill out a registration card
- ☐ show your airline tickets
- ☐ give a confirmation number
- ☐ other: ______________________

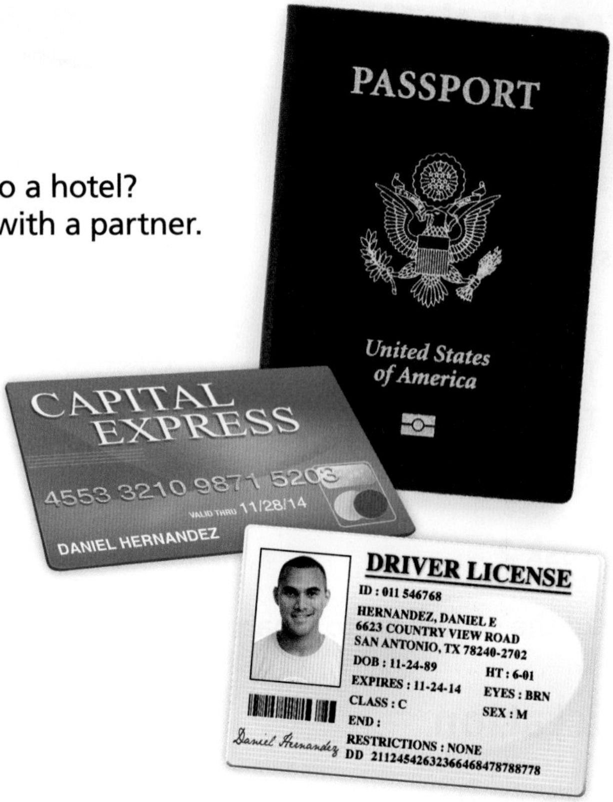

CD 3-23

Listening 1

People are checking into a hotel. What do they have to do? Listen and circle the correct answer.

1. **a.** fill out a form
   b. show a driver's license
   c. show a passport
   d. pay a deposit
   e. give the receptionist his credit card

2. **a.** give the confirmation number
   b. show a driver's license
   c. show a passport
   d. pay cash for the room
   e. leave a deposit

3. **a.** spell her name
   b. show a driver's license
   c. show an airline ticket
   d. fill out a registration form
   e. sign a card

4. **a.** show a company ID
   b. show a passport
   c. give the receptionist her credit card
   d. fill out a card
   e. leave a deposit

Listening 2

CD 3-24 ▶ Task 1

What kind of room does each guest want? Listen and check (✓) the correct answer.

1. ☑ single ☐ double
   ☐ standard ☐ deluxe
   ☐ garden view ☐ city view
2. ☐ single ☐ double
   ☐ standard ☐ deluxe
   ☐ garden view ☐ city view
3. ☐ single ☐ double
   ☐ standard ☐ deluxe
   ☐ garden view ☐ city view
4. ☐ single ☐ double
   ☐ standard ☐ deluxe
   ☐ garden view ☐ city view

CD 3-24 ▶ Task 2

Listen again. What else does each guest request? Circle the correct answer.

1. **a.** where to find public transportation
   (b.) a room away from the elevator
2. **a.** a fruit basket
   b. a wake-up call
3. **a.** an iron
   b. some clothes
4. **a.** coffee and sandwiches
   b. coffee and a salad

Listening 3

CD 3-25 ▶ Task 1

People are discussing their rooms. Listen and check (✓) the correct information.

1.

	Good	Not good
the size	☑	☐
the bathroom	☐	☐
the view	☐	☐
the facilities	☐	☐

2.

	Good	Not good
the size	☐	☐
the bathroom	☐	☐
the view	☐	☐
the facilities	☐	☐

3.

	Good	Not good
the size	☐	☐
the bathroom	☐	☐
the view	☐	☐
the facilities	☐	☐

4.

	Good	Not good
the size	☐	☐
the bathroom	☐	☐
the view	☐	☐
the facilities	☐	☐

CD 3-25 ▶ Task 2

Listen again. What did each guest complain about? Circle the correct answer.

1. (a.) that there was nothing in the refrigerator
   b. that the TV did not work

2. a. the size of the bathroom
   b. the mattress

3. a. the view from the window
   b. the heat in the room

4. a. the shower
   b. the stereo

Asking for confirmation

Pronunciation

Intonation for confirming information

Pronunciation Help

Use rising intonation to ask a question that confirms information.

CD 3-26 ▶ Task 1

Listen and repeat.

1. A: My name is Pennington. B: Did you say "Pennington"?
2. A: I'd like a single room. B: Excuse me. Did you say "a single" room?
3. A: I need to see your passport. B: I'm sorry. Did you say you need to see my passport?

▶ Task 2

Read the sentences to a partner. One student is A, and the other student is B.

Dictation

CD 3-27 ▶ Task 1

Listen to the conversation. Write the missing words.

A: Yes, sir, may I help you?

B: I'd like a room for two nights, please.

A: __________ __________?

B: That's right. My name is Chris Smithson.

A: Did you __________ __________?

B: No, Smithson. S-M-I-T-H-S-O-N. Do you need to see some identification?

A: __________ __________ __________ you have identification?

B: Yes. I do. Here you go.

▶ Task 2

Practice the conversation with a partner. Be sure to use the correct intonation.

Conversation

Work in pairs. Imagine you are checking into a hotel. Think about the information you will need to check in. Take turns being a receptionist and a guest.

UNIT 22

Traffic

Getting Ready

Match the pictures with the descriptions. Write the correct letter next to each description. Compare your answers with a partner.

A. 

B. 

C. 

D. 

1. Road repair ____
2. Two cars in a collision ____
3. Traffic congestion on a freeway __A__
4. Traffic moving smoothly on a freeway ____

CD 3-28 Listening 1

People are making announcements about traffic conditions. Listen and number the pictures.

A. 

B. 

C. 

D. 

E. 

F. 

Listening 2

CD 3-29 ▶ Task 1

These people have to go somewhere. How will each person get there? Listen and circle the correct answer.

1. a. by bus
   (b.) by car
   c. by bicycle

2. a. by car
   b. by bus
   c. by subway

3. a. by taxi
   b. by car
   c. by bus

4. a. by car
   b. by bus
   c. by taxi

5. a. by car
   b. by taxi and subway
   c. by subway and on foot

6. a. by car
   b. by bike
   c. by bus

CD 3-29 ▶ Task 2

Listen again. Are these statements true or false? Check (✓) the correct answer.

	True	False
1. There is a big baseball game today.	☐	☑
2. There is a traffic jam on the freeway.	☐	☐
3. Taxis usually don't come very quickly.	☐	☐
4. Kevin lives close to Harry.	☐	☐
5. The traffic is backing up because a traffic light is broken.	☐	☐
6. The weather is not so good.	☐	☐

Listening 3

CD 3-30 ▶ Task 1

People are describing solutions to traffic problems in their cities. What did each city do? Listen and circle the correct answer.

1. (a.) They improved the quality of buses.
   b. They raised bus fares on weekends.
   c. They lowered taxi fares.

2. a. They built more parking garages.
   b. They made drivers pay a daily fee.
   c. They kept all cars out of the city center.

3. a. They made many streets downtown one-way.
   b. They made new lanes for cars to use.
   c. They made a law that people can drive downtown every day if they have a special pass.

4. a. They did not allow people to ride a bicycle downtown.
   b. They made a rule that there must be at least three people in a car to go downtown.
   c. They bought new buses that don't create pollution.

CD 3-30 ▶ Task 2

Listen again. What problem did each city have? Write the correct letter.

1. __c__   a. The traffic moved too slowly.
2. _____   b. There weren't enough parking spaces.
3. _____   c. The public transportation wasn't very good.
4. _____   d. The air pollution in the city needed to be lowered.

Describing problems

Pronunciation

Contractions of *there is/has* and *there are*

Pronunciation Help	
How we spell it	**How we say it**
there's	therez
there are	therer

CD 3-31 ▶ Task 1

Listen and repeat.

1. *There's* a lot of traffic.
2. *There's* a collision.
3. *There's* been an accident.
4. *There's* been a problem.
5. *There are* two stalled cars.
6. *There are* some improvements.

▶ Task 2

Read the sentences to a partner. Be sure to pronounce *there is/has* and *there are* as contractions.

Dictation

CD 3-32 ▶ Task 1

Listen to the conversation. Write the missing words.

A: Are you going downtown today?

B: Yes, but __________ __________ marathon today. There's going to be a lot of traffic.

A: Yes. __________ __________ several streets blocked off.

B: And I just heard there's been an accident, too.

A: It's true. There's been a collision __________ __________ __________.

B: Wow! So, I guess I'll walk. __________ __________ __________ with my feet today!

▶ Task 2

Practice the conversation with a partner. Be sure to pronounce *there is/has* and *there are* as contractions.

Conversation

Work with a partner. Think about the best way to get around your town or city. Ask and answer questions about traffic and transportation in your town or city.

UNIT 23

Roommates

Getting Ready

Look at the picture. What kind of roommate is this person?

What are some important qualities of a roommate? Check (✓) the four most important qualities and add another of your own. Compare your answers with a partner.

- ☐ good-tempered
- ☐ good cook
- ☐ doesn't snore
- ☐ reliable
- ☐ studious
- ☐ sociable
- ☐ thoughtful
- ☐ sense of humor
- ☐ quiet
- ☐ talkative
- ☐ neat
- ☐ considerate
- ☐ other: ______________________

CD 3-33 Listening 1

People are talking about their roommates. Listen and circle the two words that best describe each person.

1. (**a.**) considerate
b. messy
c. helpful
d. unreliable

2. a. unfriendly
b. talkative
c. studious
d. generous

3. a. messy
b. studious
c. sociable
d. humorous

4. a. unreliable
b. inconsiderate
c. neat
d. helpful

5. a. neat
b. sociable
c. considerate
d. studious

6. a. lazy
b. quiet
c. studious
d. bad-tempered

Listening 2

CD 3-34 ▶ Task 1

People are comparing their new roommate with their old roommate. Which one does each person prefer? Listen and check (✓) the correct answer.

	The new one	The old one
1.	☑	☐
2.	☐	☐
3.	☐	☐
4.	☐	☐
5.	☐	☐
6.	☐	☐

CD 3-34 ▶ Task 2

Listen again. What word or phrase describes each person's favorite roommate? Write the correct letter.

1. _e_ **a.** considerate

2. ____ **b.** humorous

3. ____ **c.** neat and clean

4. ____ **d.** thoughtful

5. ____ **e.** not too talkative

6. ____ **f.** friendly and happy

Listening 3

CD 3-35 ▶ Task 1

People left voicemails for their roommates. What do they want their roommates to do? Listen and circle the correct answer.

1. a. make the bed
   b. lend him a book
   (c.) bring him a book

2. a. invite her friends over
   b. buy some snacks
   c. make some snacks

3. a. call his parents
   b. make restaurant reservations
   c. clean the living room

4. a. buy some food
   b. clean the room
   c. empty out the refrigerator

CD 3-35 ▶ Task 2

Listen again. Are these statements true or false? Check (✓) the correct answer.

	True	False
1. Ted did not make his bed this morning.	☑	☐
2. Meg invited friends over to play games.	☐	☐
3. John is going to buy dinner for Ken.	☐	☐
4. Carrie forgot to clean the apartment.	☐	☐

Conversation Corner Describing people

Pronunciation

Word stress for emphasis

Pronunciation Help

Stress the words that add emphasis in a statement.

CD 3-36 ▶ Task 1

Listen and repeat.

1. He's réally smart. 2. He's extrémely noisy. 3. She's térribly rude! 4. She was véry considerate.

CD 3-37 ▶ Task 2

Listen. Mark the stressed words in the sentences. Then read the sentences to a partner.

1. They talk réally loudly. 2. She is extremely forgetful! 3. We're very quiet.

Dictation

CD 3-38 ▶ Task 1

Listen to the conversation. Write the missing words.

A: How do you like your new roommate?

B: I don't know . . . She's __________ __________!

A: What do you mean?

B: She's __________ __________ at night. She watches TV and sings in her room.

A: So she's not as nice as your last roommate?

B: No. My last roommate was __________ __________ and considerate.

A: So what are you going to do?

B: Well, you know me. I'm __________ __________. I guess I won't do anything!

▶ Task 2

Practice the conversation with a partner. Be sure to stress the words used for emphasis.

Conversation

Work with a partner. Think of four words to describe one of your friends.
Then take turns describing your friend to your partner.

UNIT 24

Travel

Getting Ready

Which of these have ever happened to you on vacation? Check (✓) your answers and compare them with a partner.

	Yes	No
You missed a flight.	☐	☐
Someone stole your money.	☐	☐
You lost your wallet.	☐	☐
You lost your passport.	☐	☐
Your bags didn't arrive.	☐	☐
You got sick.	☐	☐
You ran out of money.	☐	☐

CD 3-39 Listening 1

Emily is talking about her vacation. Listen and number the pictures.

A. ☐

B. 1

C. ☐

D. ☐

E. ☐

F. ☐

Listening 2

CD 3-40 ▶ Task 1

People are calling home while they are on vacation.
Listen and check (✓) the word that describes each person.

1. Jill
   - [ ] worried
   - [x] excited
   - [ ] upset

2. Sean
   - [ ] relaxed
   - [ ] happy
   - [ ] frightened

3. John
   - [ ] relaxed
   - [ ] pleased
   - [ ] worried

4. Rachel
   - [ ] happy
   - [ ] sick
   - [ ] excited

5. Mary
   - [ ] upset
   - [ ] sick
   - [ ] relaxed

6. Meg
   - [ ] bored
   - [ ] pleased
   - [ ] angry

CD 3-40 ▶ Task 2

Listen again. Why does each person call? Circle the correct answer.

1. Jill ___________.
   (a.) has met someone interesting
   b. was in a dangerous situation
   c. wants to ask a favor

2. Sean ___________.
   a. isn't having a good time
   b. has some news
   c. needs money

3. John ___________.
   a. lost his wallet
   b. lost his ticket
   c. will be coming back on time

4. Rachel ___________.
   a. has good news
   b. needs help
   c. told her friend about a health problem

5. Mary ___________.
   a. lost her glasses
   b. was in an accident
   c. has bad news

6. Meg ___________.
   a. is coming home earlier
   b. is taking a different flight
   c. doesn't have anything to do

Listening 3

CD 3-41 ▶ Task 1

People are describing travel experiences. Is each statement true or false? Listen and check (✓) the correct answer.

	True	False
1. Chelsea		
a. She was eating in a Korean restaurant.	☑	☐
b. She asked the woman to help her.	☐	☐
c. The woman invited her to join the family at their table.	☐	☐
d. She hasn't been in touch with the woman since then.	☐	☐
2. Brooke		
a. She was traveling by train in Italy.	☐	☐
b. Her wallet was in one of her bags.	☐	☐
c. Someone stole one of her bags.	☐	☐
d. The person didn't steal the wallet.	☐	☐
3. Steve		
a. He had extra clothes with him.	☐	☐
b. The airline did nothing to help.	☐	☐
c. His bags arrived four days later.	☐	☐
d. His bags had important things inside them.	☐	☐
4. Rachel		
a. She got sick with food poisoning in Australia.	☐	☐
b. She was only sick for two days.	☐	☐
c. She knew someone in Sydney.	☐	☐
d. She went sightseeing for three days.	☐	☐

CD 3-41 ▶ Task 2

Listen again. Why does each person want to go back again? Write the correct letter.

1. Chelsea __b__ **a.** wants to listen to the traditional music.

2. Brooke _____ **b.** wants to see a temple.

3. Steve _____ **c.** wants to see the museums.

4. Rachel _____ **d.** wants to scuba dive.

Describing a vacation

Pronunciation

Reduction of *was*

Pronunciation Help	
How we spell it	**How we say it**
was	wuz

CD 3-42 ▶ **Task 1**

Listen and repeat.

1. A: How *was* your trip? B: It *was* great.
2. A: How *was* the food? B: It *was* okay.

▶ **Task 2**

Read the questions and answers with a partner. One student is A, and one student is B.

Dictation

CD 3-43 ▶ **Task 1**

Listen to the conversation. Write the missing words.

A: Hi, Jen. __________ __________ your trip?

B: It was great! I had a wonderful time.

A: __________ __________ the food?

B: It was good! I ate a lot!

A: How __________ __________ __________ there?

B: It was beautiful the whole time I was there.

A: So what was the best thing __________ __________ __________?

B: The beaches!

▶ **Task 2**

Practice the conversation with a partner. Be sure to reduce *was*.

Conversation

Work in pairs. Think about a vacation you took. Tell your partner where you went. Ask and answer questions about what you did on your trip.

TACTICS FOR TESTING
PAGE 108

TACTICS FOR TESTING

UNITS 1 – 4
Testing focus: Focused listening

CD 4-2 Part 1

Look at the pictures. For each picture you will hear a question and four statements. Choose the statement that best matches the picture.

ANSWER SHEET

1	A	B	C	D
2	A	B	C	D
3	A	B	C	D
4	A	B	C	D
5	A	B	C	D
6	A	B	C	D
7	A	B	C	D
8	A	B	C	D
9	A	B	C	D
10	A	B	C	D
11	A	B	C	D
12	A	B	C	D
13	A	B	C	D
14	A	B	C	D
15	A	B	C	D

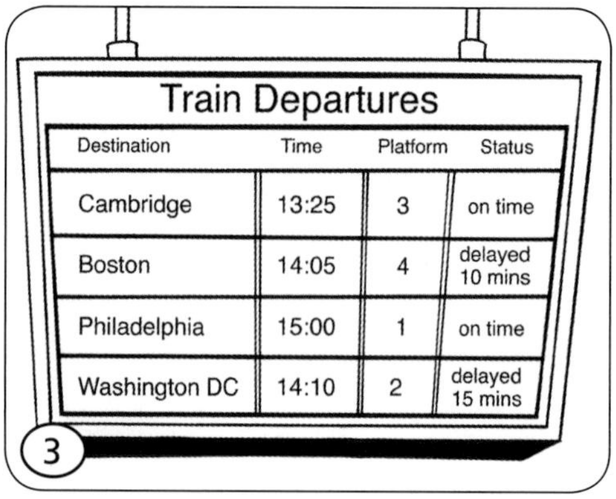
Train Departures

Destination	Time	Platform	Status
Cambridge	13:25	3	on time
Boston	14:05	4	delayed 10 mins
Philadelphia	15:00	1	on time
Washington DC	14:10	2	delayed 15 mins

CD 4-3 Part 2

Listen to each question. Choose the correct response. Use your answer sheet.

7. **A.** Oh, I met some friends and we went out for dinner.
   B. Yes, it's too bad the weekend is over.
   C. I worked all day on Monday.
   D. I think I'll stay home and relax.

8. **A.** Yes, I think it was last night.
   B. I don't really like playing games.
   C. What time does it start?
   D. No, I fell asleep on the sofa.

9. **A.** But I love classical music.
   B. Yes, it is the next station.
   C. We can take the bus from here.
   D. I think they already changed it.

10. **A.** It is a great game.
    B. It's just not my favorite.
    C. When I drive the car.
    D. It makes me want to dance.

11. **A.** He goes to the gym.
    B. I think he rented a movie.
    C. He said it's his last weekend.
    D. He's moving to a new house.

12. **A.** Yes, I had a really good time.
    B. You can bring a friend if you like.
    C. No, it's not my birthday.
    D. Sure. What kind of party is it?

CD 4-4 Part 3

Listen to the following short conversations and answer the questions below. Use your answer sheet.

13. What did the woman do on Saturday?

A. She went bowling with her boyfriend.
B. She had a boring weekend at home.
C. She met her girlfriends in the evening.
D. She stayed home and watched TV.

14. Who is the man?

A. A hotel guest
B. A passenger
C. A cyclist
D. A taxi driver

15. What does the woman say about the food?

A. She likes the cheese.
B. She made them herself.
C. She's never had goat meat before.
D. Her mother gave her the recipe.

ESTABLISH THE MAIN IDEA
When a new listening passage begins, try to establish the main idea. Establishing the main idea will help you pick out important details.

UNITS 5 – 8
Testing focus: Listening for details

CD 4-5

Part 1

Look at the pictures. For each picture you will hear four statements. Choose the statement that matches the picture. Use your answer sheet.

ANSWER SHEET

1	A	B	C	D
2	A	B	C	D
3	A	B	C	D
4	A	B	C	D
5	A	B	C	D
6	A	B	C	D
7	A	B	C	D
8	A	B	C	D
9	A	B	C	D
10	A	B	C	D
11	A	B	C	D
12	A	B	C	D
13	A	B	C	D
14	A	B	C	D
15	A	B	C	D

1

2

3

4

5

6

CD 4-6 ## Part 2

Listen to each question. Choose the correct response. Use your answer sheet.

7. **A.** I don't feel like it.
   B. That's kind of you to offer.
   C. Something quick and easy.

8. **A.** Sure, if you like.
   B. No, I'm sick of junk food.
   C. Actually, I don't eat meat.

9. **A.** I've never seen him wear that color.
   B. No, Thai food is too spicy for him.
   C. I think it's in his closet.

10. **A.** I think I like the other belt better.
    B. Oh, are we about to land?
    C. I can't go any faster.

11. **A.** I'd like to check this bag in.
    B. I work in the sales department.
    C. Can't I keep it under my seat?

12. **A.** No, the washing machine is leaking.
    B. I think I need more exercise.
    C. Yes, it's been raining all day.

CD 4-7 ## Part 3

Listen to the following conversation. Choose the correct answer for each question. Use your answer sheet.

13. **What are the speakers discussing?**
    A. Plans for an upcoming birthday
    B. What they want to do for Mother's Day
    C. A restaurant they went to last week
    D. An upcoming trip

14. **Why does the woman reject the man's first suggestion?**
    A. She doesn't like flowers.
    B. The restaurant is too expensive.
    C. She doesn't want to do the same as last year.
    D. She had forgotten the date.

15. **What can be inferred about the speakers' mother?**
    A. She went to the Imperial Hotel last year.
    B. They haven't bought her flowers before.
    C. She is difficult to satisfy.
    D. She likes to eat French food.

TAKE NOTES AS YOU LISTEN
On some tests, such as the TOEIC® test and the TOEFL® test, you will answer several questions about the same listening passage. Taking notes as you listen will help you remember details.

UNITS 9 – 12
Testing focus: Listening for organization

CD 4-8

Part 1

Choose the correct answer, A, B or C.

1. How did the man learn about the openings?
   A. He read a notice at the diner.
   B. A friend told him about it.
   C. He saw an ad in the newspaper.

2. The man is currently
   A. unemployed.
   B. working.
   C. a student.

3. What kind of relevant work experience does the man have?
   A. working under pressure
   B. dealing with customers
   C. serving

4. The man would be free to begin work at the restaurant
   A. tomorrow.
   B. next week.
   C. next month.

Complete the notes below. Write NO MORE THAN TWO WORDS AND/OR A NUMBER for each answer.

JOB OPENING AT THE AMERICAN DINER

Job
- server

Conditions
- permanent position
- one-month **(5)** ________________ period
- need to provide two **(6)** ________________

Hours of work
- two **(7)** ________________ (change every three weeks)

Days off
- **(8)** ________________ and **(9)** ________________

Benefits
- free meals and **(10)** ________________

CD 4-9 ## Part 2

Complete the sentences below. Write NO MORE THAN TWO WORDS for each answer.

11. The club is going to hold an ________________ tournament every year.

12. The club's ________________ are closed for two months every year.

13. The gym instructors can produce individual ________________ for members.

14. In the first exercise studio, there are ________________ classes.

15. Instructors are able to design ________________ which are safe and enjoyable.

16. Leisure membership does not include ________________.

Look at the map of the Thornton Sports and Leisure Club. Write the appropriate letter on the blank next to each question.

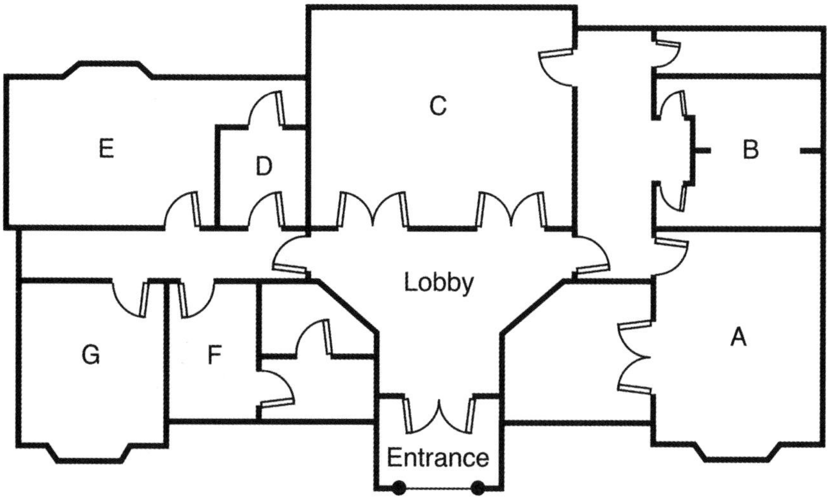

17. ____ locker rooms

18. ____ indoor pool

19. ____ members' lounge

20. ____ exercise room

LISTEN FOR TRANSITIONAL WORDS
On some tests, such as IELTS™ and the TOEFL® test, you will listen to long conversations and talks. Transitional words or phrases such as *first of all, however, then*, and *furthermore* help to organize these long passages.

TACTICS FOR TESTING

UNITS 13 – 16
Testing focus: Picture-based questions

CD 4-10

Part 1

Look at the pictures. For each picture you will hear four statements. Choose the statement that matches the picture. Use your answer sheet.

ANSWER SHEET

1	A	B	C	D
2	A	B	C	D
3	A	B	C	D
4	A	B	C	D
5	A	B	C	D
6	A	B	C	D
7	A	B	C	D
8	A	B	C	D
9	A	B	C	D
10	A	B	C	D
11	A	B	C	D
12	A	B	C	D
13	A	B	C	D
14	A	B	C	D
15	A	B	C	D

1

2

3

4

5

6

CD 4-11

Part 2

Listen to each question. Choose the correct response. Use your answer sheet.

7. **A.** I enjoy walking.
   B. I think it's just past two.
   C. No, I had to pay about $20.

8. **A.** Yes, that's correct.
   B. He collected my paper.
   C. I really like toy robots.

9. **A.** Yes, the color is perfect.
   B. Not really, it's a bit tight.
   C. It could be sweeter.

10. **A.** I don't have time to wash it.
    B. It doesn't keep time very well.
    C. I haven't watched it yet.

11. **A.** Can I get them by tomorrow?
    B. Two white ones and one blue one.
    C. I can spend up to about $40.

12. **A.** It's on Boulder Avenue.
    B. There are many theaters in the city.
    C. Nothing I haven't already seen.

CD 4-12

Part 3

Listen to the following conversation. Choose the correct answer for each question. Use your answer sheet.

13. When did the man notice the problem with his purchase?
    A. When he bought it
    B. Last week
    C. The day after he bought it
    D. Last month

14. What will the shop do if the man does not have a receipt?
    A. Give him a replacement
    B. Give him a receipt
    C. Fix the hole
    D. Give him a refund

15. What does the man want the shop to do?
    A. Return his money
    B. Repair the tent
    C. Pay for the damage
    D. Exchange it for a similar model

LISTEN FOR PREPOSITIONS
Many tests, like the TOEIC® test, have questions about the locations of objects and people in pictures. Listen carefully for prepositions of place, such as *in*, *on*, *next to*, and *between* when answering these questions.

UNITS 17 – 20
Testing focus: Listening for details

CD 4-13 Part 1

Look at the pictures. For each picture you will hear a question and four statements. Choose the statement that best matches the picture.

ANSWER SHEET

1	A	B	C	D
2	A	B	C	D
3	A	B	C	D
4	A	B	C	D
5	A	B	C	D
6	A	B	C	D
7	A	B	C	D
8	A	B	C	D
9	A	B	C	D
10	A	B	C	D
11	A	B	C	D
12	A	B	C	D
13	A	B	C	D
14	A	B	C	D
15	A	B	C	D

CD 4-14 Part 2

Listen to each short conversation. Choose the correct response. Use your answer sheet.

7. **A.** I'll go and wake him up.
   B. There isn't anyone asleep.
   C. I was terrified when I was a child.
   D. It's just the wind. Go back to sleep.

8. **A.** Can you ask him to call me back?
   B. Yes, we have one available.
   C. I don't think we can help.
   D. Sorry, I didn't receive the message.

9. **A.** I think it is locked.
   B. It was over $200.
   C. That's very kind of you.
   D. Yes, I'd love to join the club.

10. **A.** The cathedral was the best part.
    B. It was okay, but a bit expensive.
    C. Yes, I think it should be a very good day.
    D. The transportation wasn't very fast.

11. **A.** Your suitcases will need to be weighed.
    B. Just go through here to gate number 3.
    C. Okay. The shuttle bus leaves in five minutes.
    D. You'll have to check the luggage in.

12. **A.** That's right. It isn't the desk.
    B. Yes, here is your boarding pass.
    C. Please put your baggage over here.
    D. Yes, but you need to go to counter G.

CD 4-15 Part 3

Listen to the following short conversations and answer the questions below. Use your answer sheet.

13. **Why is the man upset?**
    A. He saw a snake outside.
    B. Summertime is too hot for him.
    C. There are lots of insects in the house.
    D. There's a small animal in the room.

14. **What will the man do after this conversation?**
    A. Wait for a phone call
    B. Call back later
    C. Give his number
    D. Call his friend, Bryan

15. **What is the woman's problem?**
    A. The gate for her flight has changed.
    B. Her flight has been canceled.
    C. She's lost her boarding pass.
    D. She's missed her flight.

LISTEN FOR PARAPHRASING
On many tests, correct answer choices restate information from the listening passage using different language. Only one answer is correct. Choose the answer that restates the exact information from the passage.

UNITS 21 – 24
Testing focus: Question-focused listening

CD 4-16 Part 1

Complete the form below. Write NO MORE THAN TWO WORDS AND/OR A NUMBER for each answer.

BONNINGTON HOTEL REGISTRATION FORM

Date

- 17th June

Type of room

- **(1)** ________________

Number of nights

- **(2)** ________________

Special requests

- Room overlooking the **(3)** ________________

Guest details

- Name: Mrs. G. **(4)** ________________
- Home address: **(5)** ________________
- Zip code **(6)** ________________

Payment Method

- **(7)** ________________

Choose the correct answer, A, B or C.

8. Guests who want to eat breakfast in the Washington Room have to

A. complete a request form.
B. present their registration card.
C. place an order in the evening.

9. What does the receptionist say about sending e–mails?

A. There's a good wireless signal throughout the hotel.
B. There are PCs in the hotel bedrooms.
C. Guests can rent a phone cable.

10. What is the quickest way of getting information about the local theater?

A. ask the porter
B. look on teletext
C. go to the theater

CD 4-17 ## Part 2

Complete the sentences below. Write NO MORE THAN TWO WORDS for each answer.

11. Cycling to work can save employees both money and ________________.

12. In recent years, ________________ have increased in the city.

13. Regular cycling improves health and reduces ________________.

14. If more employees cycle to work, the company needs less ________________.

15. Employees can borrow a maximum of ________________ for cycling equipment.

16. Employees are allowed to buy two bikes if part of their journey is by ________________.

Look at the map of the cycle routes below. Write the appropriate letter on the blank next to each question.

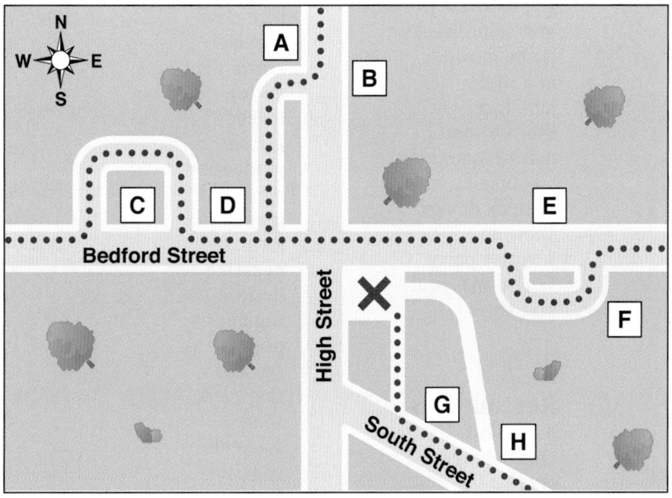

17. ____ museum

18. ____ library

19. ____ bus station

20. ____ fire station

PREPARE FOR THE TEST DAY
Don't try to study everything the night before the test. Be sure to get enough sleep and eat a healthy breakfast in the morning.

VOCABULARY INDEX

Unit 1
The Weekend
awful
beach
bodybuilder
bodybuilding
butterflies
boring
borrow
competition
contest
disappointing
downtown
enjoyable
exercise
exhausted
good-looking
mall
muscles
nephews
novel
part
pleasant
terrific
tired
tiring

ask (someone) out
closest friend
forest trail
go on a date
go to a movie
go to a nightclub
go to the gym
How come?
I'll bet!
nature walk
outdoor concert
play a sport
play computer games
pop music
pull out
science fiction
supposed to be
watch a DVD
watch TV
You're kidding!

Unit 2
City Transportation
air-conditioned
carefully
convenient
dangerously
emergency
expensive
fare
ferry
flight
passenger
reasonable
rude
safe
subway
taxi
ticket
uncomfortable

as soon as you can
Are you free?
be in a hurry
catch a train
dining car
good/poor condition
Hop in!
just me
not very often
seat belts
shuttle flight
snack bar
Where to?

Unit 3
Neighbors
anniversary
annoying
appreciate
arrogant
borrow (something)
burglar
considerate
cookout
delivered
driveway
elderly
gossip
hammer
impolite
inconsiderate
incredible
invite
mailbox
neighbor
neighborhood
normally
nosy
request
retired
return (something)
shy
spotless
upset
upstairs
wave
watching out

be off (of work)
break in
by any chance
can't stand (someone)
count on (someone)
day care
don't mind (doing something)
fit in
I can manage
mind one's own business
move in
not think much of (someone)
say "Hello"
turn up (the volume)
work long hours

Unit 4
Celebrations
anniversary
barbecue
bring
buffet
candles
chocolate
cute
delicious
grill
guest
guitar
hold
host
memorize
painted
play (musical instrument)
serve
snack
turn (20)

birthday party
blow out
felt like
got to know (someone)
grill some steaks
home movie
in a while
junk food
listen to music
make (something) yourself
potluck dinner
show up
surprise party
Why don't you…
You know

Unit 5
Restaurants
asparagus
cheeseburger
chef
Chinese (food)
convenient
décor
deserved
downtown
empty
flavor
French (food)
fries
heat (v.)
hurry
immigrants
Japanese (food)
Korean (food)
lighting
Mexican (food)
milkshake
part-time
polite
salt
server
simple
starving
Thai (food)
tip
vanilla
vegetarian

baked potato
be sick of (something)
credit card
eat out
fast food
feel like (eating something)
for a change
hot sauce
junk food
leave a tip
make sure
stay home
the only trouble
wait on (someone)
What's the occasion?
your treat

Unit 6
Gifts
already
birthdays
bracelet
convenient
cotton
elastic
glasses
graduation
imported
jewelry
local
necklace
necktie
organic
popular
present
salesclerk
shirt
souvenir
special
teapot
weddings
wrapped

allergic to (something)
awfully small
Father's Day
go with (something)
housewarming party
I wonder if…
Mother's Day
natural ingredients
Perfect!
pick (something) out
sound expensive
The price is right
think of (doing something)

Unit 7
Air Travel
board
bumpy
catch
clear
collect
crowded
dry
economy
facilities
fantastic
fasten
headphones
horrible
immigration
route
smooth
tasteless

aisle seat
business class
change my seat
check in
customs form
Do you mind…
economy class
far away
fill out
flight attendant
headphones
on time
overhead compartment
put your seat forward
safety instruction card
seat belt
seat number
seat pocket
so-so
spring break
TV screen
weather report
window seat
working properly

Unit 8
Mishaps
apology
break
charge
clogged
deserted
directions
dishwasher
dripping
drycleaner
flooded
horrified
ink
locksmith
manager
offend
offer
plumber
puddle
reschedule
ruined
soaked
soda
solution
spill (something)
suggest
tray
tricky

trip
unfortunately

catch the bus
catch the next one
checkout counter
dry out
emergency number
flat tire
get locked out
get lost
leave the water running
look (something) up
make sense
tow truck

Unit 9

Jobs

actually
architect
assistant
autograph
bags
baker
bellhop
boss
call
carry
chef
client
colleagues
commuting
chauffeur
creative
design (v.)
drive
hairdresser
invite
manager
mechanical
meetings
newspaper
online
plenty
quiet
reporter
salary
security
server
vacations

answer the phone
auto shop
cash register
change jobs
flight attendant
go pretty well
market research
take a break
TV producer
working hours

Unit 10

Keeping Fit

aerobics
beach
bicycling
courts
dangerous
diet
equipment
fat
golf
improve
indoors
jogging
lessons
operation
pool
ride
rollerblading
romantic
sit-ups
swimming
track
traffic
volleyball
weightlifting

at home
be into (something)
can't stand
club fee
get in shape
get some exercise
give up
go out
health club
lift weights
make (my knees) hurt
New Year's resolution
put on weight
take up
used to

Unit 11

Invitations

accept
actually
afterwards
bowling
bunch (of flowers)
instead
invitation
opera
plans
playing
refuse
rent
soprano

be free
be out
come over
I'd love to.
Maybe some other time.
my place
see a movie
stay home
That sounds great.

Unit 12

Campus Life

appointment
attractive
biology
boring
cafeteria
campus
cell
chemistry
classroom
competitive
crowded
draft (of a paper)
essay
experiment
genetics
grade
gym
interesting
lab
lectures
lockers
logo
major
modern
neat
outdoor
overcrowded
scan
schedule
semester
slides
stationery
unfair
unfriendly

art history
Be right back.
campus bookstore
check (a book) out
computer lab
computer science
discussion group
front row
not crazy about (something)
professor's office
sleeping in
state-of-the-art
student ID
What's the matter?

Unit 13

Hobbies and Pastimes

adventure
collecting
concerts
cooking
garage
gardening
hiking
history
hobbies
Mozart
nature
oil (paintings)
outdoors
pastimes
retired
studio
watercolor (paintings)

children's books
classical music
comic books
computer screen
eat out
except me
free time
lose interest in (something)
packed away
playing video games
public library
sit around
stamp albums
surfing the Internet

Unit 14

Shopping Problems

bargain (n.)
bargain (v.)
broken
buttons
case
camcorder
camera
damaged
exchange
faded
guarantee
heel
impossible
lock
long-sleeved
missing
receipt
refund
repair
sale
shrank
stain
sweatshirt

be out of (something)
changed color
come off
compare prices
get fed up with (something)
half the price
poorly made
sold out of (something)
wrong size

Unit 15

Hotel Services

bags
blanket
concierge
delayed
face (the street)
flight
housekeeping
lasagna
laundry
letter
light (food)
lonely
mailbox
mattress
meat
noisy
non-smoking
occupied
package
password
pressed
reservation
sauce
send (something) up
share
snowstorm
spaghetti
staff
towel
vegetarian

bell captain
Can I help you?
dry cleaned
flat-screen TV
front desk
Is there anything else?
room service
spring break
wake-up call

Unit 16

Movies

action
action-packed
animation
audience
century
chasing
comedy
cowboy
danger
disappointing
dumb
excitement
exit (n.)
fantastic
fast-moving
frightening
good-looking
handsome
hilarious
horror
horse
kidnapped
policeman
romance
scare
surprise
terrible
unbelievably
universe
vampire
western

animated movie
bank robbery
battle scene
car chase
clean up the town
come out of the ground
go crazy
How was the movie?
make people laugh
play opposite
ride a horse (v.)
science fiction
show times
soundtrack
special effects
worth the price

Unit 17

Fears
bats
biology
brake
button
coat
cockroaches
confidence
creepy
downstairs
drown
engineer
freeways
frightened
garden
heights
hose
insect
jellyfish
lab
land (n.)
mice
nearly
nervous
poisonous
realize
scream
seaweed
shark
snakes
spiders
traffic
waves

Are you afraid of anything?
be afraid of
be terrified of (something)
don't mind (something)
get on (a plane, a bus, etc.)
get stuck
knock (someone) over
roller coasters
scuba diving
step on (something)
swim laps
take care of (oneself)

Unit 18

Phone Messages
cash
deliver
extension
mailroom
neighbor
package
repair
tip (v.)

auto repair
average number
be in (to have arrived)
be in touch
boat trip
Call me.
cell phone
confirm (a flight, reservation)
credit card
dental appointment
give (someone) a call
make a phone call
memorize
pick (something) up
receive a phone call
shuttle bus
text message
travel agency

Unit 19

Touring a City
built
cemetery
charge
delicious
exhausted
gate
gifts
glamorous
grow
iron
itinerary
jokes
local
mansion
market
museums
peanuts
picnic
reasonable
religion
rink
souvenirs
stars (famous people)
stuffy
telescope
temple
tour
van
works (of art) (n.)
zoo

art museum
baseball player
be worth doing
bus tour
cultural event
How was the tour?
ice skating
places of interest
tour guide
What did you see?

Unit 20

Airports
announce
arrivals
bags
board (v.)
customs
delayed
departure
distance
efficient
escalator
facilities
fairly
flight
gate
gifts
immigration
level
monitor
parking
pleasant
restroom
souvenirs
suitcases
terminal

ATM machines
baggage claim
car rental
change a baby
check-in counters
currency exchange
department stores
duty-free shop
flight insurance
foot bridge
freshen up
game center
go through security
information counter
shopping mall
shuttle bus

Unit 21

Hotels
arrange
coffeemaker
complaint
confirmation
deluxe
deposit
double (occupancy)
electric
facilities
fan
form
hardly
identification
inconvenient
iron
mattress
mini-fridge
ordinary
passport
registration
reservation
sign (v.)
single (occupancy)
standard
tiny

as hard as a rock
at this hour
check in
confirmation number
driver's license
electrical outlet
fill out
light sleeper
May I help you?
wake-up call

Unit 22

Traffic
ambulance
announcement
annual
avoid
bike
bus
city center
collision
congestion
cyclists
display
downtown
fares
fine (n.)
freeway
government
hundreds
improvement
instead
lanes
light (traffic) (adj.)
lower
marathon
one-way
pass (a law)
pollution
quality
rates
route
smoothly
stalled
traffic
unusually

a bunch of (something)
be allowed to (do something)
broken down
bumper to bumper
drive (someone) home
give (someone) a ride
keep away from (a place)
keep (something) out
parking garage/lot
parking space
public transportation
road repair
Traffic is backing up.
traffic jam
traffic light (n.)
traffic report

Unit 23

Roommates
arguments
awful
baking
bother
chemistry
completely
considerate
good-tempered
neat
noisy
party (v.)
quiet
reliable
snacks
snore
sociable
studious
talkative
thoughtful
unreliable

a mess
be out of (something)
be over
come by
do (someone) a favor
do (something) oneself
get along
get back
go back for (something)
good cook
in case
invite (someone) over
keep the place clean
last semester
lose (one's) temper
my folks (parents)
pick up
phone bill
put something away
school work
sense of humor
wait around

Unit 24

Travel
backpack
completely
cousin
excited
flu
hole
join (someone)
lose
passport
pleased
relaxed
relaxing
remove
research
shore
slight
snorkeling
spectacular
steal
traditional
upset
vacation
volcano
wallet
waterfalls
worried

be out of money
change one's flight
cost (one) an arm and a leg
get a chance to (do something)
get sick
How was the food?
How was your trip?
hula dance
in the rush
keep in touch
miss a flight
see sights
Sorry I missed your call.
take photos
turn up